IF THE WAR COMES

◆

IF THE WAR COMES

◇

Ann Mari Wallenberg
with Philip Dodd

CLEARVIEW

First published in the UK in 2020 by Clearview Books
99 Priory Park Road, London NW6 7UX
www.clearviewbooks.com

Compilation © Clearview Books, London

Text © Celia Pilkington and Charlotte Milln

ISBN 978-1908337-528

Editorial Consultant: Philip Dodd
Design: Bernard Higton
Editor: Catharine Snow
Picture Research: Rosanna Dickinson

A CIP record of this book is available from the British Library.
Printed in the UK by Pureprint, East Sussex.

CONTENTS

❖

DRAMATIS PERSONAE

THE MACKAYS

Alexander Mackay (my maternal grandfather) was born in Dunkeld, Scotland in January 1856. One of eight children, he worked his way up from apprentice at a chartered accountants in Dundee to become the company's senior partner. He was secretary, director and Chairman of the Board of the Matador Land and Cattle Co., a founder of the Shell Oil Corporation, and also had interests in copper mining and citrus farming. He was the owner of Glencruitten House, Oban (where his Cathedral of Trees is being actively restored) and La Rochelle, Lake Alfred FL. He died in 1936, the day after fishing in the local loch. *Family nickname: Gugga Daddy.*

Dorothy Mackay (my mother). Born in 1900, she showed early interest in acting, performing as a teenager at the Theatre Royal, Glasgow in 1914. After school at Roedean she went to Newnham College, Cambridge in 1920 to study Modern and medieval Languages and English. Married Marcus Wallenberg on 22nd August 1923: they had three children: Marc, Peter and myself. After her divorce from my father, she married Charles Hambro in February 1936: together they had one daughter, Sally. After Charles Hambro died in 1963 she lived in Chelsea and Sussex until her death in 1984. *Family nickname: Doie.*

Edith Mackay née Burns (my maternal grandmother) was the daughter of Dr Robert Ferrier Burns D.D., a Presbyterian minister in Canada; Edith was born in St Catherines, Ontario. Always extremely musical, she played the organ in Fort Massey church in Halifax, Nova Scotia, one of her father's subsequent postings. While studying music in Leipzig she met Alexander Mackay: they married in October 1890 (he built an organ for her to play at Glencruitten): they had four children, including my mother Dorothy. *Family nickname: Guggsie.*

Elizabeth Mackay (my aunt). The third of the Mackay children – my mother was the youngest. She was, like my grandmother, a hugely talented musician: her principal instrument was the piano, which she studied at the Royal College of Music. She never married. *Family nickname: Peter/Auntie Pooh.*

Ferrier Mackay (my uncle), son of Alexander and Edith, born 1892. He attended Fettes College, then King's College, Cambridge where he studied mathematics, and in 1914 he married Grace Croft, a RADA-trained actress, who had appeared in the premiere of G.K Chesterton's play Magic. They had two daughters, my cousins Elizabeth (known as Weenie/Tad) and Rosemary (Ba). They spent much of their time at the Mackay family's La Rochelle house in Florida. Ferrier died in 1940 by his own hand. *Family nickname: Uncle Kay.*

Margaret Mackay (my aunt) born in Broughty Ferry, her parents' house before Glencruitten was built. Like my mother, she was educated both at Roedean and Newnham College, Cambridge, where she read Moral Sciences and agricultural studies: with her interest in forestry she was instrumental in helping Alexander plant his Cathedral of Trees at Glencruitten. In 1926 she married Lieutenant R. C. Donovan RN: they had three children, Rickard, Christopher and Fay. She later became a powerhouse in local London politics. *Family nickname: Marga.*

THE WALLENBERGS

Amalia Wallenberg née Hagdahl (my paternal grandmother) was born in 1864: her father was the physician and cookery expert Charles Emil Hagdahl, her mother his housekeeper Jacobina Ödman. She married Marcus Wallenberg in 1890 – their six children were Sonja, Jacob, Andrea, Gertrud, Ebba, and the youngest, my father Marcus. A redoubtable matriarch, she lived well into her nineties. Her birthday on 29th May is still celebrated by the family every year. *Family nickname: Farmor.*

Ann Mari Wallenberg (the author) was born in 1929 at Parkudden House in Stockholm, the third child of Marcus and Doie Wallenberg. Her observations of her childhood experiences during the Second World War are recorded in the following pages. She married Michael Bonsor in 1951, they had four children: Celia, Charlotte, Camilla and Robert and lived in London, Berkshire and Suffolk. Ann Mari died in April 2019. *Family nickname: Anis.*

Jacob Wallenberg (my uncle). His early years followed a similar pattern to my father's – naval academy, learning the banking ropes at various banks in Europe and the US, joining Stockholms Enskilda Bank as an associate director in 1918 and as CEO from 1927-1946. He was also a great sailor: all his boats were called Refanut. Although he never married, he adopted his biological son Peder, whose mother was Madeleine Sager. Jacob died in 1980 at the age of 87. *Family nickname: Finkin/Juju.*

Marc Wallenberg (my older brother) was born in June 1924 in London. He graduated from Harvard Business School in 1949, and as our father had, worked at various banks from the late 1940s, before becoming a deputy director of SEB in

1953 and CEO in 1958. He married Olga Wehtje in 1955; they had four children, Marcus, Axel, Mariana and Caroline. He died in November 1971 by his own hand, using a hunting rifle, near a lake south of Stockholm. *Family nickname: Boy-Boy.*

Marcus Wallenberg Jr. KBE, Kungliga Serafimerorden (my father). After divorcing my mother, Doie, and marrying Marianne Bernadotte, née de Geer af Leufsta, in 1936, he was part of a vital Swedish trade negotiating team during the Second World War. After the war he became CEO of Stockholms Enskilda Bank, where he had been a director since 1925, and continued in that role from 1946 to 1958. He continued his love of sailing and tennis, and was chairman of the Swedish Tennis Association from 1934 to 1953. He died in 1982 at Täcka Udden, the bank's house on Djurgården, the island in Stockholm where I was born. *Family nickname: Dodde.*

Marcus Wallenberg Sr. (my paternal grandfather). One of the twenty-one children of André Oscar Wallenberg, the founder of the Stockholms Enskilda Bank, Marcus was born in 1864, studied law and became a circuit judge in 1892, the same year his brother Knut persuaded him to join the family bank, where he was CEO from 1911 to 1920. The celebrated Swedish dish 'Wallenbergare' is named after him. He died in 1943.

Peter Wallenberg (my younger brother). My parents were based in Stockholm when Peter was born. He did not go into the family bank, but worked for the industrial company Atlas Copco in the US, Rhodesia, the Congo and the UK. He was then Chairman of Investor AB, overseeing mergers that created AstraZeneca, ABB and Stora Enso. He was married three times, with three children from his first marriage, Jacob, Andrea and Peter Jr. When he died in 2015 his final journey was in a unique hearse built by Saab, a company which his forefathers had been instrumental in founding. *Family nickname: Pirre.*

THE HAMBROS

Sir Charles Hambro KBE, MC (my stepfather). By the time he married my mother in 1936 – his first wife Pamela Cobbold, had died in her very early 30s – Charles Hambro had not only been working for Hambros Bank, the family business, since 1920, but had been appointed a director of the Bank of England at the age of 30. He joined the Special Operations Executive at the outbreak of the Second World War looking after Scandinavian operations, and was made head of SOE in 1942, resigning a year later: he was knighted for his SOE work. He died in London in 1963, aged 65.

Charlie Hambro, Baron Hambro (my stepbrother) was a year or so younger than me, born in July 1930. He joined Hambros Bank in 1952 and was in turn Managing Director, Deputy Chairman and then Chairman from 1972. He was senior honorary treasurer of the Conservative Party in the 1990s, for which he received a life peerage in 1994, taking the title Baron Hambro of Dixton and Dumbleton. He married twice, having three children, Clare, Charles and Alexander with his first wife Rose Cotterell and gaining a stepdaughter when he married Cherry Huggins. He died in 2002.

Pamela Hambro (my youngest stepsister). After our wartime adventures in the US, and her enforced break with Bob Pennoyer, Pammie married Robin Lowe in 1945 (and had a son Ian) and following their divorce Andrew Gibson-Watt in 1951: Andrew's brother David Gibson-Watt was already married to Pamela's older sister, Diana. Pamela and Andrew had three children, Martin, Rosalind and James. Widowed in 2006, she died in 2015.

Sally Hambro (my half-sister) was born in 1938, my mother's fourth child and Charles Hambro's fifth: she was barely a toddler when we were dispatched to the US in 1940. Her first husband was Peter Snow: they had three children, Catharine (who is publishing this book!), Sara-Rose and Alexander. She later married Anthony Brand, the 6th Viscount Hampden, a stockbroker and merchant banker who ran his inherited estates at Glynde in the Sussex Downs near Lewes until his death in 2008.

THE MORGANS

Catherine Morgan, known as 'Catty', was 21 when she married Henry Sturgis Morgan one week after he graduated from Harvard. The daughter of Herbert Hoover's Secretary of the Navy, she brought some serious American history along with her: she was descended from two US Presidents, John Adams and John Quincy Adams, the 2nd and 6th Presidents respectively.

Harry Morgan was born in London in 1900, where his father John Pierpoint (J.P.) Morgan Jr was working. After Harvard he joined J.P. Morgan and co-founded Morgan Stanley in 1935. With his wife Catherine he had five children – all boys. He was trustee, president and chairman of the Morgan Library and Museum, and chairman of the America's Cup Committee.

Harry Morgan Jr, the eldest of Catherine and Harry Morgan's five boys, followed his father to Groton and Harvard, joining the US Navy in 1942 and going on to have a long and distinguished naval career, commanding a series of battleships and serving as Commander of Naval Services in Korea in the 1970s, ending with the rank of Rear-Admiral. He had four children with his first wife Fanny, and later married Jean, the sister of Senator John McCain.

Bob Pennoyer's mother Frances was a Morgan, the daughter of J.P. Morgan Jr. After his painful parting from my stepsister Pammie in 1943 he served in the US Navy in the Pacific. After the war he graduated from Columbia Law School, and was a federal lawyer before joining a private practice, where he was always committed to public service. He married Vicky Parsons in 1948: they had four children. In his nineties, Bob still goes to his law office in Manhattan every day.

◇

FOREWORD

THIS IS THE story of my life, and in the main the first 21 years of it, when I found myself part of three extraordinary families, the Mackays, the Wallenbergs and the Hambros. I was not always at the heart of those families, in fact I was frequently peripheral, which often led me to question my true identity, but made me something of an objective observer of the worlds they moved in, worlds that for the most part have evaporated. I was also caught up in the flurry of global events during the Second World War, and looking back I am faintly astonished to find myself still here at 89 and able to reflect on my good fortune at surviving.

One of the characters who makes a cameo appearance in these pages, Sir Victor Mallet, who was the British Ambassador to Sweden when war broke out, wrote an unpublished memoir which is in the vaults of the Churchill Archives in Cambridge. In it he writes, 'If the word "memoir" is to be taken literally this is a memoir, because I am writing almost entirely from memory.' Although I have been able to corroborate my story through cross-checking, wherever possible, other sources, much of it went undocumented, or the documents that might have existed have vanished, in fires, blitzes, or in one house move or another.

Memory, of course is a fickle beast, with all its idiosyncratic quirks, kinks and confusions. So this is what happened to me - to the very best of my memory.

INTRODUCTION

$\mathbf{M}$Y PARENTS MET at sea in November 1922, travelling from Southampton to New York onboard the Cunard Line's RMS *Mauretania*, one of the most romantic and glamorous transatlantic liners of the day, holder of the coveted Blue Riband.

How they ever met was extraordinary, a miracle, a fairy tale. F. Scott Fitzgerald would have had a field day with the story.

My mother was just 22, on her way across the Atlantic to visit her father, who was over in the United States on business. My father was only a year older, heading out to New York to spend time working at the First National City Bank.

They found themselves thrown together for the seemingly endless days of the crossing, and by the time the *Mauretania* had docked in New York Harbour, they had decided they were going to get engaged – but had as yet not told anyone else.

He was Marcus Wallenberg, a scion of the Wallenberg banking family, one of Sweden's most powerful business dynasties. Charming – deceptively charming, ominously charming – and dashing, he was a brilliant, if erratic, tennis player who a few months earlier in the summer had made his first appearance at Wimbledon.

Marcus was really rather good-looking (even if I say so myself: the photographs of him from the time capture all of that surface sparkle) and the adored youngest son of six children, doted on by his mother.

He was quite a catch, I imagine.

She was Dorothy Mackay, known as Doie, the daughter of Alexander Mackay, an entrepreneurial and rather extraordinary Scottish businessman. An accountant by training, he had become a founding director of Shell Petroleum, and had interests in cattle in Texas and an orange plantation in Florida. So although the family home was Glencruitten, an estate in the hills above Oban, on the west coast of Scotland, all of the Mackay family were used to crossing the Atlantic. If they had had air miles for liner travel, the Mackays would have been multi-platinum card holders.

In fact, at one point, Cunard threw a special party to thank them for all their custom over the years. I can certainly remember as a young girl watching the huge cabin trunks being prepared for the voyage. Some pieces of luggage were virtually the size of wardrobes, full of evening gowns, with drawers stuffed with accessories and niceties, others the most petite of vanity cases. They were piled up in the front hall of Glencruitten, a number of them tantalisingly labelled 'Not Wanted On Voyage', ready to be loaded up for the trip.

This was definitely first class travel, and their fellow passengers were drawn from the upper echelons of European and American society. When my mother sailed to New York the year before, in October 1921, with her elder brother Ferrier – on board the SS *Olympic*, a sister ship of the *Titanic* – they were joined by Claire Dux, an opera singer who had played Mimi opposite Caruso, the Russian violinist Bronislaw Huberman, Beatrice Countess of Granard, an American heiress whose husband was Master of the Horse for George V, and Professor Hans Christian Jacobaeus, a Swedish physician who was a pioneer of keyhole surgery.

Neither my mother or father ever told me about the exact moment when they were first attracted to each other on the *Mauretania*. What I always knew they had in common was a tremendous sense of fun. They were both charismatic, both extrovert, even though my mother had a very strong streak of seriousness alongside the frivolity: she had studied English and German language and literature at Newnham College, Cambridge (in those days when women were allowed to study but naturally could not, God forbid, receive a degree for their efforts).

From the outside it might seem that Marcus was the more sophisticated of the two of them, a successful international sportsman and favoured son, my mother an innocent wee Scots lass ready to be snared. But in fact, what I have come to realise over time is that she was the sophisticated one, my father the *ingénu*. Both of them were supremely immature, of course.

Compared to the Mackays' familiarity with travelling, Marcus Wallenberg was new to the whole experience. My mother had made the journey to America many times; this was the first time he had travelled that far from home. She was a *bona fide* intellectual; he had read very little other than banking reports and perhaps the sports pages. Doie, I imagine, was quite a daunting prospect.

Two months later, Marcus wrote a letter to his parents describing Doie Mackay. She was, he reported, 'Strong and shapely with a nice, perhaps even pretty, face framed by blonde hair, from the centre of which peeks a pair of blue eyes.' He praised her 'high spirits, good health and a good demeanour... spirited and alert'.

After landing in New York, they continued to see each other, which reinforced their decision to marry. Marcus was introduced to the Mackays that Christmas at La Rochelle, the family's bungalow in Lake Alfred, Florida, and Doie's parents gave – we don't know how willingly – their blessing to the couple.

Marcus's letter describing Doie's virtues and explaining they were now engaged took a somewhat circuitous route to Sweden, forwarded via various locations, and only reached his parents in February 1923. In the meantime Alexander Mackay – assuming that Marcus's family would be fully up to date with events – had dispatched a cable suggesting a meeting. Marcus Wallenberg Senior, completely ignorant of who the sender was, and why on earth he wanted to arrange a meeting, sent a terse cable by return 'NO! WHO ARE YOU?'

When Marcus's letter eventually arrived, his father was obliged to send a far more conciliatory communication to the Mackays, which led to a get-together of both families on neutral ground in Paris. Marcus Sr wrote to his son Jacob that Alexander Mackay was 'an old-fashioned, solid Scottish businessman with a wide education. The mother is the daughter of a Scottish clergyman with an interest in music. The daughter is a modern type of girl with little screwed-up eyes, mostly on the defensive. Of course, Dodde [my father's family nickname], with his excellent prospects, should have managed a more advantageous match, although he could probably also have got himself into something far worse.' Faint praise, indeed.

The Wallenbergs were important and significant in Swedish society, but Marcus Sr had no idea how they were viewed by the Mackays. Sweden, to them, was some Godforsaken, rather backward country on the Northern limits of the civilised world, an outlandish, mythical place like Lapland. For the Wallenbergs, on the other hand, Scotland, especially the Highlands, equally represented some kind of remote outpost.

Four months after the Paris summit, my parents were married in Oban on 22nd August 1923. The reception was held in the 'beautiful and picturesque grounds of Glencruitten' on the sloping terraced lawn in front of the house – and was enhanced by a production of the ancient Celtic tragedy, *Deirdre Of The Sorrows*, a performance which was directed by my uncle, Doie's brother Ferrier.

And so that chance meeting on the *Mauretania*, only nine months earlier, had led to a union between the 'mad Mackays' – a nickname used by one of my step-sisters – and 'the Wallybags'. And I am here as living proof.

◇

CHAPTER ONE

◇

THE MACKAYS OF GLENCRUITTEN

Glencruitten House, Oban, Argyll in 1936.

I F I clambered up out of a small window in one of the top-floor turrets, I could squeeze myself up onto the lofty roof of Glencruitten, the house in Scotland that belonged to my mother's family, the Mackays.

As a five-year-old, that difficult ascent was made significantly easier by my older brothers and cousins who, already up on the roof, would helpfully give me a powerful tug up through the window. Once outside the going was, to say the least, treacherous. A foot placed on a precarious gutter was all that protected us from slipping and falling to our doom. We ignored the danger, and instead admired the view.

From this eyrie I could look down and across the Glencruitten estate and the forest of trees, thousands of them, that my grandfather had planted. Beyond, over the bay of Oban and a sliver of silver sea, you could make out the island of Mull on a clear day. In the other direction, Ben Cruachan, the largest hill in the area, was permanently snow-capped, even in summer.

Somewhere below, hidden by the trees on the steep hillside tumbling away from the house, was the small coastal town of Oban, set around the bay, surrounded by wood-covered hillsides and sheltered from the wilder excesses of the seas by the Isle of Kerrara.

Down there in Oban was St Columba Church, where my parents had been married, and the harbour, where the Royal Navy frequently docked for some well-deserved rest and recuperation, livening up the local social scene no end.

Glencruitten was where I spent every summer with my mother and brothers. During the rest of the year we lived in Sweden, my father's country, but from June onwards we would decamp to Scotland. In fact it had been part of my parents' marriage contract – pre-nuptial agreements are nothing new – that we would spend six weeks and more there every summer, a clause specified and introduced, I believe, by my Scottish grandfather Alexander Mackay to ensure that his daughter and grandchildren would always return home once a year.

He knew that my father's family, the Wallenbergs, were as powerful and strong-willed as he and his own family were. This was a crafty way of making sure the balance in the relationship was not completely lopsided. However, my father, although happy to let his wife and children comply with that requirement, rarely accompanied us. He preferred to stay in Sweden, spending his time sailing or indulging in other leisure pursuits.

Glencruitten, an imposing baronial-style property, had been acquired shortly before the end of the First World War by my grandfather, and under his guidance, altered and adapted by Sir Robert Lorimer, who was known as the 'Scottish Lutyens'. My grandfather was interested in architecture throughout his life, an interest I have always shared.

The house was a suitable manifestation of the success Alexander had achieved as a clever, ambitious and imaginative businessman who had come from humble beginnings. He was gregarious, shrewd and had real imagination.

His branch of the Mackays were a large crofting family (he was one of eight brothers and sisters) in Sutherland, one of the very northernmost parts of Scotland. At a time when the railways were barely starting to reach that far, he nonetheless walked all the way from Sutherland to Dundee – then the closest station on the new line – to look for work. It was an indication that he had bags of initiative and even more stamina.

Edith (Gugsie) and Alexander (Gugga Daddy) Mackay
at Glencruitten, 1923.

Although he was unable to get a proper education, he read widely, and sought out engineers and scientists to talk to as that was one of his interests. Apprenticed to a firm of chartered accountants in Dundee, he channelled his persistence and ambition into working his way up to becoming a partner. His ambition was not sated, only stimulated. He was described as 'a gregarious man, a wise judge of character and someone with a great breadth of vision'.

He began to look towards wider horizons. In the 1880s he became involved with opportunities in America, including cattle ranching in Texas with, at the time, one of the biggest herds of Hereford cattle in the world. The Matador Land & Cattle Co. was founded by some Dundee businessmen in 1882. Alexander was appointed Secretary: he rose to be Chairman.

One of his fellow Matador directors was Murdo Mackenzie, a fellow Scot, who moved to Colorado in 1885. Murdo Mackenzie was known as the most influential cattleman in America: a 1922 press profile wrote, 'He is heavy-set. Physically, he is a man whom it would be hard to move. And when he looks straight at you out of big grey eyes, you cannot doubt that it would be harder still to move him from a course of action which he had decided was right.' Murdo and Alexander formed a redoubtable partnership.

Alexander was also one of the founding directors of the Shell Union Oil Co. in Texas, and had business interests in Arizona (mainly copper mines) and Florida.

His stamina remained unquenchable. His annual trips to America involved heading from Dundee to Liverpool, sailing across the Atlantic to New York (where Mackay Irons had offices), then taking a train to Chicago, where his cattle were driven up from Texas for slaughtering, across to Oklahoma and finally to his ranch near Amarillo across prairie fields on rutted tracks, 'which are rather trying', he said, 'to the stranger on a springless buckboard'.

Home at this point was Rocknowe House, in Broughty Ferry, just outside Dundee – a former fishing village, it was now the site of villas built for the businessmen who had made fortunes out of jute, one of the three core businesses of Dundee ('jute, jam and journalism'). He would be back home after work at 5.30 prompt, so he could spend time with his children, playing outside, reading stories, writing them little poems. When a fire, possibly caused by an electrical fault, burnt Rocknowe down in 1915 or 16, he started looking for a new property, especially one where he could cultivate trees.

The year before, he had bought 128 acres of land on the shores of Lake Rochelle in the Lake Alfred district of Tampa, Florida, a region spattered with multiple lakes, known locally as 'the chain of lakes'. There he drained the swamp – which was full of alligators – and it became his American base. This was not a vanity Stateside residence; it was also a business, as it came with a citrus grove. Alexander purchased another one thousand acres and planted more groves which produced orange juice for sale, and profit.

Alexander ordered up a house for La Rochelle. I had always thought that this had come from the pages of the Army & Navy Stores catalogue: this was the house that every British colonial who was sent out to India chose, the original flat pack. In fact it was built for Alexander in 1917 in what was called the 'Craftsman' style: the American equivalent of the Arts and Crafts movement. The style featured low-pitched roofs, overhanging eaves, with porches underneath: the roofs were supported by distinctive

La Rochelle, built on the shores of Lake Rochelle, Tampa, Florida 1923.

square columns. On hot summer nights, before air conditioning became the norm, the porches were good for sleeping on to get the coolness of the night-time air. Around the house were 112 acres of gardens laid out by John Morley, a botanist: there was a sunken garden, an arbour – and beyond that over 1000 acres containing the all-important citrus groves.

The manufacturers said the building would last for twenty years, but no one else thought the Lake Alfred house would amount to much. That house, I am pleased to report, is still standing – and is now a museum.

That's probably down to the fact that unlike most 'kit houses' – which were produced by companies like Sears & Roebuck or Montgomery Ward, who dispatched pre-fabricated sections to be bolted together – La Rochelle was from the Craftsman Company who supplied architectural plans (ours was Plan #185) which local builders and carpenters could interpret. That ties in with my impression of my grandfather: he really was a modern, far-thinking fellow.

In fact Alexander went one step further, privately hiring the architect from the Craftsman Company, George E. Fowler, to travel down to Lake Alfred and amend the plans on site, increasing the frontage onto the lake and adding a whole extra wing. The construction work on La Rochelle was completed on 10th November 1917, and the first meal served in the house was a Thanksgiving luncheon at the end of the month for Alexander, his brother John and some friends.

And so from then on the Mackay family made an annual excursion to America, ostensibly for Alexander to run their businesses in the States, but perhaps wisely they were able to spend time in Florida and avoid the worst excesses of a Scottish winter (*dreich* is the word that perfectly captures those bleak months north of the border). However, the Atlantic crossings were far from relaxing. They were often traumatic: one of my cousins remembers the family complaining that they were seasick the whole way across.

Summers at Glencruitten were a different matter: a magical season of liberty and entertainment, although the lengthy Scottish evenings were somewhat lost on me as we children were promptly packed off to bed at 6pm. After the rest of the year in Sweden, this was a chance for me to spend time with my grandfather and grandmother, my uncle and aunts: the Mackays of Glencruitten. After her marriage to Marcus Wallenberg my mother had relocated with him to Stockholm. Just as they were for me, her visits to Glencruitten were moments when she could reconnect with and imbibe the true Mackay spirit.

We did not stay in the main house. Robert Lorimer had constructed a somewhat quirky, cottagey bungalow in the grounds of Glencruitten, a short distance up the main drive towards the hills, a place which we called 'The Bungey'. Extraordinary from the outside, the insides of the bungalow were in fact quite impractical, with tiny bedrooms shoehorned up into the eaves and mahogany-seated loos sloping back in an alarming fashion, following a doctor's advice that this was the best way to cure chronic constipation. Here we stayed with our own household, including a cook and nanny.

The main house was imposing and grand. Robert Lorimer had overseen much of the detailing of the interior décor, including the furniture and lighting. In an anteroom to the library was an octagonal table incorporating a display space for precious items. On top of this stood – actually stood is too static a word, maybe floated – a statuette of Isadora Duncan, the dancer, an object which fascinated me as a child. Many years later, when the contents of Glencruitten were being auctioned off, I thought long and hard about bidding for Isadora, but sadly her price was far off the scale. I did nevertheless retrieve a bronze light from one of the passageways which now illuminates my house, although it is so vast that only one part of it dangles below the ceiling.

One downside of the summers were the mealtimes. For breakfast every day I was given a boiled egg, which arrived with a runny, and to me totally unappetising, white. I would sit in my chair and refuse to eat it. Back in Sweden we had a very kind and sympathetic maid who would clear the table and whittle away any food I left, pretending to the rest of the world I had eaten it. However in Scotland – where our nanny, also from Sweden, was ruthless – there was, sadly, no way I was going to get away with it. Eventually I would be force-fed this hideously runny egg after which I was promptly sick, and in the end, thankfully, they stopped that particular torture. At lunchtime I despised, with equal hatred, spinach; this resulted in another hour or more of stand-off in a battle of wills, a contest I would invariably lose.

Outside mealtimes, we children were pretty much left to our own devices, which was rather fun. I remember being thrown into the freezing sea off Oban and being taught to swim in icy cold water. Nowadays I can't imagine any child would even deign to be plunged into such an

Summer tennis at Glencruitten, back row from left to right: Marc 'Boy Boy'
Wallenberg, a friend of Marga's, Marga Donovan, Vera Forest, Doie Wallenberg,
Vera's mother Tella. Front row left to right: Fay Donovan, Chris Donovan, Ferrier
Mackay Jr, Peter Wallenberg, Ann Mari Wallenberg.

unwelcoming environment. I also recall almost permanent good weather,
although it must have poured with rain often. Memory can play tricks
on you like that.

We saw plenty of our grandparents, although almost never at meals
since they did not want us seated at their table. We rarely saw our mother.
When the Navy came to Oban the family would hold fantastic parties in
the big house and she was always on hand, and in glittering good form.

My brothers and I revered my grandfather (as did my father, even
though he was only an infrequent visitor). Alexander Mackay was a tall,
handsome man, who liked to wear a kilt. His demeanour might have
been off-putting, but he was immensely kind to his grandchildren, a
kindness highlighted by his slight Scottish accent. He was also extremely
intellectual. My mother had been brought up in an environment of serious
political and religious discussion. The children were encouraged to debate.
They would fight, argue, slam doors.

This was all applauded: it fostered energy and originality and character. The family were mad keen on education, definitely a Scottish trait. After school at Roedean, my mother, Dorothy – always known in the family as 'Doie', pronounced to rhyme with 'joy' – went to Newnham College, Cambridge in October 1918 to read Modern and Medieval Languages, before swapping to English.

Here she met Frances Partridge, who later became a member of the the Bloomsbury Group. At the time Frances – then Frances Marshall – had arrived from Bedales, a liberal, co-educational school, light years away from Roedean's austere single-sex environment. She wanted to go to Cambridge because her best friend, Julia Strachey, had been to Newnham.

She remembered that, 'The rules were strict at Cambridge. The First War was coming to an end, and the rules dated from before that. I had a brother who had been in prison in Germany through the war. He wasn't allowed to come for tea without a chaperone.' As Mary Hamilton, who wrote an informal history of Newnham, put it, 'Males penetrated into the College as lecturers and tutors; as visitors, they were only admitted when a bored don sat by as a gooseberry.' Finally, and especially in the months following the Armistice of November 1918, men were returning to Cambridge. One of the College reports proclaimed that 'The sap of youth and energy is running very strong'.

Doie and Frances struck up a close friendship, possibly because my mother's elder sister Margaret was already at Newnham, as was Frances's sister Eleanor: maybe they suggested their younger sisters should meet up. They became fast friends, and I am sure that they influenced each other. Frances said that Cambridge gave her 'a distinct set of values: pacifist, atheist, women's rights. Rather dull, I'm afraid I didn't change very much...' One biography of Frances Partridge describes my mother as 'a lively, funny Scottish girl with fair hair and pink cheeks'.

Life there was a mixture of the intense and the frivolous. Frances 'joined the Moral Sciences Club, which was rather romantic, mostly men crouching round a fire and smoking pipes, and tying themselves in knots while they considered problems like why the French King had no beard'.

Frances Marshall (left) and Dorothy Mackay (right) in Dorothy's rooms
at Newnham College, Cambridge 1921.

But equally there were weekly dance clubs: my mother and Frances were founders of the Quinguaginta Club, which danced to jazz. They played lacrosse for Newnham ('Miss Mackay did some surprisingly good work on the wing', says one report). And there was a regular Debating Society: in the college magazines, my mother crops up supporting the Labour Party point of view in a 1919 debate called 'The Railway Strike was unjustifiable'.

One of the reasons that my father might have chosen not to come for the summers in Scotland was that he did not feel particularly in tune with the literary, musical and artistic interests of the Mackays. That was a shame. The Mackay family all adored my father, to begin with. They said he was so good with people, full of charm and fun. My aunt once told me that you could not help liking him because he made everything fun. They used to dress up, put on plays. But alongside the fun Glencruitten was imbued with the atmosphere of intense discussion and debate, and he may have found that found off-putting.

The artistic side of the Mackays was led by my grandmother, whom we called Gugsie (grandfather Alexander was Gugga Daddy). She was a complete eccentric. Family stories were plentiful. Travelling on the train in America, she was known to have laid down after a meal flat out in the corridor so that the waiters had to step over her on the way to serve other passengers. The house was often full of visiting missionaries. Alexander bore all her fads and fancies with benign tolerance.

She was née Burns, another great Scottish family, and her father had been a Presbyterian clergyman of Nova Scotia in Canada. She was also a talented musician, who had been personally taught by Franz Liszt in Germany during the 1860s. For her benefit the library at Glencruitten contained a gigantic pipe organ.

Despite her musical skills, Gugsie had nonetheless no sense of time. Hopeless at organising the household, she luckily had a brilliant cook. She cared nothing about her clothes and her stockings were always falling down. Gugsie was totally scatty, but had a great sense of humour; and we loved her dearly.

She was very religious. The Mackays were low Church, very dull: you weren't allowed to go out and play on Sundays, you just read the bible and sang hymns, but we didn't mind with her accompanying us on the lovely organ. Sport was also central to life at Glencruitten: there were squash and tennis courts at Glencruitten (my father must have loved that). In fact the whole family was mad about tennis, and at the house in Florida there were yet more courts.

My mother was a complete mix of her parents. She had a great sense of humour, though never as scatty as Gugsie, and a serious side like her father. She loved world affairs and poetry, especially that of Keats and Shelley, and could recite reams of Shakespeare.

Her time at Cambridge had been extremely influential. This was a time when it was extremely unusual for women to go to university, full stop – and even then, they were only awarded a 'titular' degree: it took until 1948 for them to be able to receive the full degree they had worked for, and deserved. Even Charles Darwin, of all people, had written that he

The Bishop of Argyll (Alexander Mackay was a generous benefactor of
St Columba's Cathedral following Doie's wedding there), Peter Wallenberg,
Marc Wallenberg and Alexander Mackay, 1931.

thought women were morally superior, but intellectually inferior. There
was constant chaperoning of students: university life for women was, like
the rest of society, severely constrained.

Doie's brother, Robert Ferrier, the oldest of the Mackay children,
was born in 1892. He was a brilliant intellectual who went from Fettes
to King's College, Cambridge to read mathematics. Ferrier was a lovely
man, extremely clever, a brilliant mathematician. As children we adored
him as an uncle, calling him Uncle Kay. He was a loner, working all night
and sleeping during the day. You are either a lark or an owl; Ferrier – like
me – was an owl.

He never possessed a house of his own, and lived with my grandparents
for the whole of his life. Alexander Mackay wanted his family to be around
him all the time, which is why he never let Ferrier off the leash.

The four Mackay siblings in 1904, from left to right: Robert Ferrier, Margaret, Elizabeth and Dorothy.

Ferrier had been required to marry his wife, Grace, an actress, because she was having their child. But it was never a happy marriage. When the dreadful news was unveiled, sometime during the First World War, my grandmother went to inspect this girl. The family must have been quite snobbish towards Grace: an actress, good grief, the youngest of 19 children whose father, a solicitor, pronounced at her birth, 'We will now say Grace', signalling the end of his procreation.

Grace was a talented actress. She had studied at RADA – winning a gold medal there in 1910 – appeared in *Magic*, a G.K. Chesterton play, performed with both Henry Irving and Ellen Terry, and taught elocution to a teenage Flora Robson. In Dame Flora's autobiography she writes about the 'beautiful Miss Croft. She really likes money' – and that was definitely true. Ferrier may well have been a stage door Johnny before their relationship evolved.

Ferrier and Grace had two daughters, Rosemary and Elizabeth. Rosemary never married but was a great beauty. As an adult she floated downstairs, possibly fortified by her regular six o'clock Martini, until the day she died. My father knew her well – and said she was perfectly normal – but every breakfast time her mother or father would ask her 'What did you dream about last night, darling?', which in his opinion is why she went a bit funny. She made movies, and wrote film scripts, but later a bunch of letters revealed that she was taken away and given shock treatment in a hospital in Northampton: normal then, barbaric now.

My two Mackay aunts were very influential. Margaret, or Marga, the eldest of the three sisters, also went to Cambridge and studied forestry. She worked with her father on the Glencruitten estate. He was mad about trees and created a Cathedral of Trees in 1921, including pews and choir stalls, as a memorial to the First World War, laid out in the form of a St Andrew's cross – Glencruitten was on the pilgrimage route from St Andrew's to Iona. Marga married a naval officer, Rickard Donovan, whose family owned the Ballymore Estate in County Wexford.

Marga was another very forceful character: she didn't think much of the Swedes, saying rather unfairly they were 'philistines', only because they did not share the same tastes as her in music, art and academia. She thought my father's family was entirely focused around the acquisition of money. My mother used to argue with my father along the same lines. 'What about the arts?', she would demand. 'Go and find some artists and bring them to the house', he would retort.

My younger aunt Elizabeth – known as Peter (or Auntie Pooh) – was a brilliant pianist who studied at the Royal College of Music. There were two grand pianos in the drawing room at Glencruitten, where she played duets with my grandmother. That generation of women, clearly immensely talented, could have carved out extraordinary careers but never did. Why? Probably because they never had to work, and so chose not to. Between spending the summer in Glencruitten and wintering among the orange groves of Florida, there was little incentive to do anything else.

I do like the Mackay half of me. At one level it is almost overwhelming: all these strong, strong characters, but often frustrated, or never liberated, so intense and intellectual.

My aunt Marga wrote in a letter once, 'Far from home one feels mighty Scottish'. I love my Mackay roots, but to be honest I often feel rather stateless, because my mixed Swedish and Scottish heritage sometimes makes it impossible to feel completely at home in either place.

At back: Gugsie (seated), Grace Mackay, Rosemary 'Ba' Mackay, Alexander 'Gugga Daddy' Mackay (seated), unknown standing. Middle row: unknown boy, Auntie Pooh with Fay Donovan on knee, Ferrier Mackay, Doie Wallenberg holding

...nn Mari, Elizabeth 'Tad' Mackay (above), Rickard Donovan holding Chris Donovan.
Lower and bottom rows: Marc Wallenberg, Richard Donovan (lowered head),
Willie Burns (older man) Peter Wallenberg, unknown youth next to W. Burns.

CHAPTER TWO

◇

THE WALLENBERGS OF STOCKHOLM

Malmvik manor, Lindö, Uppland.

EVERY YEAR May 29th marked my Swedish grandmother Amalia's birthday. The days were continuing to lengthen before midsummer, and this particular day was celebrated, as it has continued to be for over 110 years, with a formal evening dinner at Amalia's house, Malmvik, not far from the royal palace of Drottningholm. Only the intervention of war ever stopped these dinners forming a completely unbroken sequence. The dinner is still held today, with over 70 guests.

As a small child I would be allowed to attend, sitting at a special table for the junior members of the family. It was an impressive evening, originally started when some of Amalia's elder son Jacob's friends – a flotilla of naval officers, whom she affectionately dubbed 'the codfish' – had organised a relatively intime meal at her house. She was very taken with all these splendid, dashing chaps, and the dinner evolved into a regular event and a family tradition. "What life and hullabaloo", she remembered in later years.

The dinner was held at the family house, which to a child was somewhat alarming. It had originally been an 18th-century square Swedish house, which in the 1880s one great-aunt had turned into a Scottish baronial style property, actually quite hideous, a pink version of Glencruitten.

The guests arrived at 6.30 in the evening for a 7.00 start. People always came fashionably early in Sweden, and still do. Formal dress was the code. At one point in the 1970s, the rule was relaxed, but recently the latest generation of Wallenbergs have reverted to black tie and evening gowns, which looks so much better.

My grandmother and grandfather, as host and hostess, would greet their guests in the hall. A queue began to form once the guests turned up, and then each of the new arrivals had to go back along the existing line of guests to introduce themselves in turn. My own very English husband found this an immensely annoying protocol and would simply walk back down the line muttering, 'Scrambled eggs'...

In the dining room, a photograph of my grandmother stood next to a silver bowl full of the lily of the valley that grew wild and abundant nearby – like the flowers carpeting snowdrop groves and bluebell woods in Britain. This represented significant endeavour: the result of hours of work, picking the flowers.

The menu was unvarying, and each meal was scrupulously logged and recorded in detail year after year. There were no caterers; everything was made on site by the cook. We always started with gravlax, prepared in the Swedish way, with the salmon cured with salt and dill and weighted down for at least three days, then served with creamed spinach and a poached egg.

This was followed by a mousse of game, probably roe deer, shot during the previous year and somehow preserved in an era before the deep freeze. This was accompanied with a creamy mushroom sauce made from local, wild 'cauliflower' mushrooms. Then we ate white asparagus, not the green variant, but a typical Swedish spring vegetable, served with soft whipped butter. I should note here that food was always an integral part of Wallenberg life – we are still known throughout the Swedish world as foodies – and that there is even a dish, quite well-known in Sweden, called 'Wallenbergare', supposedly created and named for my grandfather either by Charles Emil Hagdahl or by Julius Carlsson, a *chef de cuisine* at the Cecil restaurant in Stockholm: it consists of a mixture of veal, cream and egg yolk, all coated in breadcrumbs, and often served with peas and potato mash. As a dessert we had jelly created in a mould made from the leftover lees of the wine and champagne from previous dinners. This was something of a hit or miss affair, sometimes awful, often delicious, at times on a hot evening melting to the point of reverting to the original wine, or if not hard and intractable like a wine-filled football.

The drinks would start with champagne and move on to wonderful red wines. For a small child this cornucopia of food and drink, topped off with elegant guests and meticulous glamour, was intoxicating in its own right. Somewhere along the way, Wallenberg tales, traditions and myths would be re-told and relayed to the next generation.

The evening might end at 2am, and in later years, whenever I was staying in the house, I could not go to bed until the last of the guests had left. The sense of tradition was, and still is, the whole point. Families celebrate their existence in different ways. This was, and is, the Wallenberg way. The family motto is 'Esse Non Videri', to act, not just seem to be acting. Being pleased with yourself was frowned upon.

The Wallenbergs – at the time my parents got married – were already a powerful, prominent family. Just as Alexander Mackay's family had been crofters, the Wallenbergs were originally peasants from the province of Östergötland, a hundred miles or so south of Stockholm. The first upward swing of their social mobility was through one Jacob Persson, who in the early 18th century became a Royal Constable in the province and changed his name to Wallberg.

The second step-up came via the church. Two Wallberg brothers trained as Lutheran priests and went to the university at Uppsala. There was a further name change, to Wallenberg, and a son of one of these, who was the son of Marcus Wallenberg the Lutheran priest, was appointed Bishop of Linköping. The bishop's son, my great-grandfather André Oscar Wallenberg, founded the Stockholms Enskilda Bank in 1856, and steered it through some tricky waters, sailing close to bankruptcy during a recession in the late 1870s, but recovering to leave it in quite good order to his son Knut - the oldest surviving son of André Oscar's twenty-one children by three mothers – on his death in 1886.

For 25 years Knut oversaw the evolution of the bank, staying independent at a time when other banks were merging, keeping control within the Wallenberg family. Sweden had previously been a totally agrarian country which rapidly became industrial. A company which specialised in mining iron ore had been taken over by the bank, and the family's riches, and along with it increasing power, flowed directly from those seams. Knut, my great-uncle, was Sweden's Minister for Foreign Affairs. Two of his brothers, Gustaf and Axel, were ambassadors to Constantinople and Washington; another, Oscar, was head of the Swedish Tobacco Monopoly.

Knut, who did not have any children, persuaded his younger brother Marcus to leave his law studies and take up banking, thus securing the succession. This Marcus was my grandfather and his youngest son, his sixth child, was my father.

Young Marcus was much loved by his mother Amalia. She was the daughter of Charles Emil Hagdahl, an intellectual, inventive, academic doctor and agriculturalist who was mad about cattle. He invented a way to separate milk from cream, and also had the brilliant, simple, idea of turning cows around so that rather than staring blankly at a wall they looked towards the activity of the outside world. Their yields increased significantly.

He also wrote a well-respected cookery book based on his great love of food, something I have inherited but which my Scottish mother, who had been brought up on a diet of haggis and mince, never fully understood. His book, *Kok-konsten som vetenskap och konst* or *The Art of Cookery, as a Science and an Art*, allowed him to bring together his interests in science and cuisine (he was once called 'the Swedish Brillat-Savarin', a Scandinavian equivalent of the great French gastronome). However his prose was often quite lyrical. Here he is describing *surströmming*, fermented Baltic herring, considered one of the most putrid-smelling foods in the world: '*Surströmming* is an old preparation, which nature itself has always taken care of ever since the creation of the world. Our first parents caught the scent of it just outside the gates of Paradise...'

Charles's wife Emilia died in 1857, and he formed a relationship with his housekeeper, Jacobina Ödman. Amalia and her sister Johanna were the children of Charles and Jacobina, and she had been boarded out to other families before returning to her father's house in the early 1880s as a 'foster child'. Here she started moving in a different level of social circles and at one ball in 1883, hosted by André Oscar Wallenberg, she was noticed by Marcus Wallenberg. The connection was strong enough for Marcus to write to his sister (who was staying at a convent school near Tours, a requirement for the Wallenberg daughters) and say that Amalia Hagdahl had 'caught his eye'. However, it was seven years before they were married.

Despite all these successful characters in the earlier generations, my grandmother Amalia was by far the dominant figure in the Wallenberg family. My father, as the spoilt (especially in the view of his elder siblings) youngest child, was obstinate and difficult, and took after her. Both of them were temperamental, highly opinionated; a biography of my father describes him as 'argumentative and strong-willed from an early age'. Both felt they could win every argument, which led to many clashes. My father, already keen on tennis as a child, spent his time bashing a tennis ball against a mirror in his room. My grandmother took the mirror out and replaced it with a painting. My father simply moved his tennis practice to another room. Fifteen-love.

Amalia, whom I called Farmor, literally 'father's mother', was rather a beauty: a portrait of her in her late thirties, by the society painter Anders Zorn, captures her perfectly. It is quite probable that she had not wanted to marry my grandfather (she had apparently been in love with a penniless, hence unsuitable, army lieutenant).

My grandfather, who was born in the same year as her – 1864 – was a very serious, even austere, man. He worked long hours, and was noted for his devotion to the family business, and his complete, incorruptible, honesty. He once wrote, 'I believe that what commands respect is doing one's duty.'

My grandfather was always nice if rather remote to us grandchildren. My mother always got on well with him. He appealed to her serious side.

Amalia Wallenberg with her children in 1906. Left to right: Andrea, Gertrud,
Sonja, Marcus Jr, Amalia, Ebba and Jacob.

Amalia was extremely strict, particularly with her own daughters, who
had terrible childhoods: she far preferred men. However, she was always
absolutely charming to me, and had a tremendous sense of humour.
Whenever I spent time with her, we would head off to the cake shops and
eat masses of cake and ice cream.

My father's four sisters, despite being under Amalia's cosh, turned out
to be equally amusing. Sonja, the eldest of the sisters was extremely bright,
very intellectual, although once again not allowed to pursue the academic
career that would have suited her. She wanted to study languages, perhaps
at Uppsala, but instead was sent to a multi-centre finishing school: Paris,
Baden-Baden (for home economics lessons) and Oxford.

Andrea was more domesticated, a witty, wise old bird, and a formidable
sailor and huntswoman. I once shared a room with her when I was 16

or so. We talked the entire night. She told me that the sisters had been brought up to believe that their father and brothers were marvellous and knew everything, but in the end, she observed, 'you have to sort everything out yourself'. She married an olde worlde aristocrat and, perhaps surprisingly, treated him very badly.

The third of the sisters, Gertrud, married an Austrian count, Ferdinand Arco auf Valley, who was overtly anti-Nazi, and after arrest by the Gestapo spent time in the Dachau concentration camp before being released on the orders of Hermann Göring. My aunt, in Paris at the time of his arrest, was protected courtesy of her Swedish passport and its implied neutrality.

Gertrud and the Count were separated, and after the war she relocated to a residence on the avenue de Grande Bretagne in Monte Carlo to live as a tax exile, a great character – despite the collapse of her marriage, she was quite happy to retain her title as the Countess Arco – with an extremely acid tongue. When I was 17 she looked me up and down before one of the annual dinners and said, 'I see you have lipstick on. You didn't have any on last year. Take it off!' When my husband met Gertrud he, on the other hand, thought her very glamorous (she always wore beautiful outfits) and he admired that acid wit, whereas I had been frightened by it.

The youngest sister, Ebba, was a typical 1920s flapper, but also a feisty, spirited character (in fact, my uncle Jacob thought she was the most talented of all his siblings), who married a 40-something Count and Crown Equerry, Carl Bonde, despite being dispatched off by the family to Tokyo to get over her initial infatuation with him. The Wallenbergs always understood the art of marrying well.

Nicknames were endemic in the Wallenberg family. Andrea was known as Nunne, Gertrud as Calle, my uncle Jacob as Finkin. My father – the baby brother, born in October 1899 – was variously Finkelin, Dåsing and, particularly, Dodde.

My father's family also had a house on Strandvägen on one of the fashionable waterfronts in Stockholm, and a summer residence called Villa Furubo on the coast at Saltsjöbaden. However my father spent many of his early teenage summers in Germany, learning the language

Above: the Villa Furubo, Marcus Wallenberg Sr's summer house in Saltsjöbaden.
Below, from left to right: Amalia, Marcus Sr, Andrea, Gertrud and Marcus Jr.

and playing tennis. He was a fine sportsman, taller than the average Swede, and athletic. The 1912 Olympics had been held in Stockholm and enthused many young chaps like him to take up sport. My father was good at bandy – a precursor of ice hockey – but particularly strong at tennis, then almost exclusively an upper-class sport, simply because of the cost of building and maintaining lawn courts.

His uncle, my great-uncle, Axel had been the first-ever Chairman of the Swedish Tennis Association (his wife Elsa was a top tennis player and represented Sweden in the 1908 London Olympics). Axel smoothed the way for my father, who won the Swedish Schools Championship in 1917, and became Swedish Men's Singles champion three years later – by chance the *nom de guerre* or *de terrain* he chose to compete under was Macke...

He was simultaneously being groomed to take up a role in the bank. His and his older brother's first names – Marcus and Jacob – were a clear indication of their prime positions within the succession of the Wallenberg family.

At eighteen Marcus was enrolled in the Stockholm School of Economics, and at 21 he began his formal professional training, sent to work at banks in Geneva, London – at Lazard Bros – and, as we know, in America, where he was overseeing foreign securities transactions that Jacob had set up. The difference between Jacob and my father was summed up by Hans Munck, one of the bank's directors: 'For Jacob money is a goal, for Dodde a means'.

My father's biography says 'it was evident that MW had many talents; he had energy, powers of concentration and receptiveness. He was extrovert, social and practical.' He was, it says, torn between his acceptance of assuming his place within the family hierarchy and a natural 'thirst for activity'.

A favourite activity was travelling round on a motorbike. In 1919 one of his companions was Alice Hay, whose father was the Lord Chamberlain in Waiting at the Swedish court, and managing director of one of Sweden's largest companies. The relationship developed and Marcus and Alice were secretly engaged. However my grandfather advised caution, and suggested he wait before making any lasting commitment. 'A marriage', he wrote, 'is not only based upon a fancy'. Marcus acquiesced and departed on his work studies and travels for two years, at the end of which he wrote a letter to Alice cauterising any chance of a future. 'Man lives, learns, develops and changes.' Alice after waiting patiently, was, to say the least, not best pleased.

Soon after Marcus was embarking on the *Mauretania* – leaving Southampton on 18th November 1922. Amongst his fellow passengers were my uncle Robert Ferrier Mackay, his wife Grace, their two daughters, and Ferrier's sister – Dorothy.

My grandmother's house, Malmvik, with all its gables, towers and spires, is still in the family. My brother had at one point intended to live there, but although the house is by the vast Lake Mälaren, he wanted to be by the sea. One of my nephews now lives there.

I returned recently, to find much had changed. The dining room was full of children's toys and easels. The vast reception hall had been divided up into a small box room to protect the family against the cold. The wallpaper of huge flowers of silver and black – frankly rather ghastly – had thankfully been replaced. But the essence of Malmvik was still there. The huge kitchens, which I remembered as enormous, dark, full of servants and large black stoves, had the original fireplace and ovens.

As a child I had always found the whole house rather alarming and extremely gloomy – but maybe that was simply a reflection of the state of my parents' marriage.

◇

◇

CHAPTER THREE

THE MARCUS WALLENBERG JR'S

Marcus Wallenberg Jr and Dorothy Mackay on their wedding day,
Wednesday 22nd August 1923, at Glencruitten.

I STILL HAVE a, now slightly yellowed, copy of the *Oban Times* from August 1923, with a full-page report of my parents' wedding. It is a truly gigantic newspaper, the size of a small travel rug, behind which a member of the Royal Highland Yacht Club could have dropped off to sleep quite happily following a perusal of its contents after lunch.

The bride, Dorothy Helen, the article relates, is the daughter of Mr & Mrs Alexander Mackay of Glencruitten, her father 'rather widely and favourably known as a man of many important undertakings', a senior partner in Mackay, Irons & Co of Dundee, London and New York, President of Matador Land & Cattle Co – the largest herd of cattle in the United States – and a director of the Anglo-Egyptian Oil Company and the Shell Oil Company: an impressive list for that offspring of crofting stock.

Doie's groom was 'Marcus, younger son of Mr Marcus Wallenberg, vice-chairman of Stockholm Enskilda Bank, founded in 1856'. The prominence of the Wallenberg family is underscored by reference to Marcus's uncles: Knut, Sweden's Minister for Foreign Affairs during the First World War, Gustaf and Axel, ministers at Constantinople and Washington respectively, and Oscar, head of the Swedish Tobacco Monopoly. Guests included the Swedish prime minster of the day, Ernst Trygger.

There is a brief summary of Marcus's time as an officer in the Swedish Artillery Reserve and his tennis career, not least representing Sweden against Scotland in Edinburgh the year before. He is, the *Oban Times* writes, 'studying international banking', with a degree from the Stockholm School of Economics. Tellingly, and typically for the era, there is not one single mention about my mother going to Cambridge University. There is, however, a lengthy description of her 'medieval dress of silver tissue, draped on side with a cluster of arum lilies' and the 'wedding crown used by the Wallenberg family, over a white lace veil.' Her new mother-in-law Amalia Wallenberg was there in a grey charmeuse gown with a grey silk overlay and diamante embroidering. Ferrier and Grace's daughters, Rosemary and Elizabeth, were bridesmaids.

The article is illustrated by a pair of black and white photos of the bride and groom. My mother looks extremely young, as indeed she was. She is glancing sideways and maybe apprehensively at the camera, whereas my father is confidently looking directly into the lens. I showed this photograph to a friend, who was struck not only by my father's film-star good looks – he has the classical features and luxuriant hair of a matinee idol, and my goodness, doesn't he know it – she immediately commented how much he looked like one of my nephews whom she had recently met.

Although secretly the Mackays were rather appalled by the marriage, because they considered Sweden to be somewhat backwards in comparison with Britain, the wedding and reception had been a major event in Oban's social calendar. The Swedish prime minister and his wife were witnesses, and the list of wedding presents was suitably prestigious, including a motor car from my Mackay grandfather, and a Steinway grand piano given by Knut Wallenberg and his wife Alice.

The month after their wedding, Marcus and Doie returned to Sweden and then headed on to New York, where my father was going to enter the next stage of his formal training for the bank, working at Brown Brothers & Co. In Ulf Olsson's biography of my father, *Furthering A Fortune*, he writes succinctly that the newly weds 'would live a fairly nomadic life for the next three and a half years'.

The Wedding Party, standing left to right: Rickard Donovan, Margaret (Marga) Donovan, Ferrier Mackay, Jacob Wallenberg, Elizabeth (Peter) Mackay, Carl Björnstjerna (husband of Marcus's elder sister Sonja).
Seated left to right: Marcus Wallenberg, Rosemary (Ba) Mackay, Doie Mackay, Elizabeth (Tad) Mackay.

THE OBAN TIMES, SATURDAY, AUGUST

PICTURESQUE WEDDING

MARC WALLENBERG. — DOROTHY H. MACKAY.

Top right: The *Oban Times*, August 1923, with details of Marcus and Doie Wallenberg's wedding.
Above: The wedding cake, placed in the dining room at Glencruitten.

It may have been a nomadic lifestyle, but it was still extremely luxurious. In an echo of the transatlantic journey on which they had first met, my parents travelled from Southampton to New York on another Cunard liner. This time they took the RMS *Aquitania*, the third of a trio of express liners, following the *Mauretania* and the ill-starred *Lusitania*, the sinking of which – torpedoed off the south coast of Ireland by a German U-Boat in May 1915, with the loss of nearly 1,200 passengers and crew – had significantly tilted American public opinion towards taking part in the war.

After the stint in New York and some time spent travelling around the States, Marcus and Doie returned to Britain the following spring, in May 1924, on board the SS *Olympic* – a sister ship to the *Titanic* – so that Marcus could work in the international business department at Hambros Bank in London. The Wallenbergs knew the Hambro family well, not least because they had an interest in the bank, and one of the Hambro sons, Charles, had also sailed with *his* new bride, Pamela, to New York on the SS *Majestic*, so that he could gain experience at J.P. Morgan. Harry Morgan of that family knew Marcus well; they both loved sailing. In the close circle of banking families, the younger generation socialised constantly.

Somewhere in the middle of this my mother found time to give birth to their first child, my older brother Marc, in June 1924 in London, shortly before Marcus was dispatched to Crédit Lyonnais in Paris later that summer (he and Doie had an apartment on the boulevard Pereire in the 17th *arrondissement*).

It was a brief intermission, as they were then moving to Berlin in 1925 where they would frequently see both the Hambros and the Morgans, as well as members of the Wallenberg family. Marcus was by now an Assistant Managing Director, the equivalent of being a Vice-President, of the Wallenberg bank.

He was dutifully paying his dues and making his way up the ranks – but still able to play plenty of tennis, appearing on Centre Court during the 1925 Wimbledon Championships, the first Swede ever to do so, and a pioneer of that illustrious line of Borg, Edberg, Wilander & co. who

Marcus Wallenberg Jr playing in the Davis Cup semi-finals, 1926.

would follow. His secret weapons were a powerful volley and a relentless competitive streak.

When they were living in Paris he practised twice a week with René Lacoste, and became good friends with Jean Borotra, the 'Bounding Basque' – Lacoste and Borotra were two of France's 'Four Musketeers' who dominated Wimbledon in the mid-1920s. In July 1926 Marcus was a member of the Swedish team who made it through to the semi-finals of the International Lawn Tennis Championships (now the Davis Cup), where they lost in a whitewash to France's Musketeers. This was no disgrace as the French had not lost a single match during the entire competition: my father at least managed to take the first set against Borotra. The other Swedish team member was Sune Malmström, who also worked in banking: a history of Swedish tennis rather waspishly notes that 'they noted their notorious losses in neat columns'.

Earlier that year Marcus had helped popularise tennis in Sweden by taking part in an exhibition match at the Nya Tennishallen against the Czech player Jan Kozeluh (himself a Wimbledon quarter-finalist) in front of King Gustav V and his children – my mother and grandfather, Marcus Sr, were sitting alongside them in the Royal Box. In the press coverage, my father was considered to be 'a player of international standing': a realistic description – he was clearly no slouch on the courts. The 'speed, verve and security' of his strokes belied his 'alleged inconsistency'.

That 1926 Davis Cup semi-final turned out to be the highlight of his career, however, as shortly afterwards he was forced to give up tennis completely, suffering from a debilitating lung problem. He did make one short comeback, but that was that, and from then on he concentrated on keep-fit exercise instead, and continued to promote tennis as the chairman of the Swedish Tennis Association.

Doie meanwhile was trying hard to endear herself to her Wallenberg in-laws. With her innate language skills, she was quick to become fluent in Swedish. Most of the Wallenbergs, who as a rule were somewhat stiff and stuffy, loved Doie instantly. She was always attempting to lighten the atmosphere when she went to their houses, suggesting games of charades or other parlour games.

Not everyone was seduced, though, however much she tried to out-charm Marcus. She wrote hilarious letters to her siblings, telling stories of when she first went to stay in Sweden, staying in Marcus's parents' house, where they were stuck in separate bedrooms, miles from each other, and she had to amuse herself while Marcus played bridge with his father for hours into the night. Things were exacerbated by the fact that Marcus's mother Amalia, did not get on with my mother at all, and was really rather unkind to her. In exactly the same way as the Mackays had not approved of Doie marrying a Swede, Amalia, who only ever spoke Swedish, was, at least initially, furious that her cherished film star of a youngest son had chosen a Scottish girl; she did not want a foreigner in the family.

The *Ilderim*, Marcus Wallenberg Jr's yacht.

However well they liked Doie, the Wallenbergs truly knew nothing about the Mackays and vice versa. We eventually held a large get-together of both families in 2017 so that finally, finally, they could do just that: get to know each other. One of my cousins gave a presentation about the Mackays to explain who we actually were...

Although he was perfectly happy to winter with the Mackays in Florida, playing tennis on the clay courts, going out in boats on the lake, riding the horses there, my father did not enjoy going to Glencruitten in the summer, preferring to stay in Sweden, hunting and shooting or sailing late into the lengthy evenings. He was a tremendous sailor, who much later part took part in the 1936 Berlin Olympics, and then in the Coppa d'Italia, the European championships for 8-metre yachts, challenging amongst others the German and Italian teams with his yacht *Athena*. He won the title in 1938, and defended it in 1939 with another yacht *Ilderim* (the Turkish word for Thunderbolt, his favourite name for all his boats from then on). My mother did not like sailing 'at all'.

Around this time my father had also become something of an amateur movie director; many of the films he shot are still in existence: reels from their time in Berlin, showing evenings spent in clubs, all the women in cloche hats. But what my mother later told me she remembered was the terrible poverty in post-war Berlin, people walking in bare feet, pushing wheelbarrows of the increasingly valueless money, simply to buy a loaf of bread. She felt guilty because she was foreign, and she was not suffering.

In May 1926, a second son, my brother Peter was born, in Stockholm: his birthday, the 29th May, was exactly the same as my grandmother Amalia's, so he always said that he never had a birthday because it was always hers. However, the bonus was that when Peter was born on her birthday, Amalia thawed immediately, completely changing in her attitude to Doie and thereafter devoted to my mother.

Finally, after the peripatetic start to their marriage my parents settled in Sweden in Autumn 1926, moving into a villa called Parkudden, which had been re-built at the turn of the century for Baron Carl von Essen, the husband of Marcus's aunt Ruth. The family had struck a deal with the Royal Administration of Djurgården to rent the villa, which was not far from the summer house of Knut, my great-uncle. A short walk away was the residence of the banker and art collector Ernest Thiel: now a permanent museum, Thielska Galleriet.

'Settled' is far too permanent a term, however. The villa was not yet ready for them, and required a complete overhaul and renovation. So they stayed in a hotel in Stockholm, but almost straightaway, were off again – to Nice, and Algeria: this time not for banking reasons but to alleviate my father's lung problems. My young brothers stayed behind with the family in Stockholm.

This constant travelling greatly concerned Marcus's mother Amalia and she persuaded Doie to come back in the early part of 1927; my father returned a little later. There were, apparently, already rumours of blazing rows between Doie and Marcus: and the long times they spent apart were deemed to be neither a good thing nor helpful in the least.

Whenever Doie was at Parkudden, true to her mantra that 'there's more to life than business', she invited similarly minded creatives, artists and writers to visit. She was a keen amateur actress (in 1914 she had even performed at the Theatre Royal in Glasgow).

By September 1928, when Doie was pregnant for a third time, Marcus was as busy as ever. As his biographer says, 'Doie had discovered early in their marriage her husband's single-mindedness and determination'.

Appointed to the Directorate of the Bank in 1927, he was now getting deeply involved in the industrial ownership activities of the SEB: the bank would take on struggling companies or oversee the development of what we would now call start-ups with a view to them becoming long-term clients. During their stay in the US, Marcus had been inspired by visiting Niagara Falls, and so led the bank's involvement with Asea (a Swedish electrical company). In 1928 he was made a director of AB Atlas Diesel. After he had sorted out some problems they were going through it flourished and is now Atlas Copco, a huge global industrial group.

Later that year my parents received an invitation to go to New York, for the December wedding of Count Folke Bernadotte, one of King Gustav V's nephews, to Estelle Manville, the daughter of an American industrialist. This was a huge social event, held at the Episcopal Church of St John in Pleasantville, New York. The *New York Times* described it as 'one of the most brilliant society gatherings in recent years'. The church 'sparkled as decorations, jewels and dress flashed in the light of hundreds of candles'. Estelle's veil was topped off by a tiny nine-pointed coronet of diamonds, which had been commissioned from the Swedish court jeweller. My mother, in the early stages of another pregnancy, had not felt well enough to travel, so once again my father went alone, and had a whale of a time with the other guests, including the groom's brother Carl Bernadotte and his wife Marianne.

Six months after that glittering wedding, I make my first active appearance in this book... A Tuesday's child, and so meant to be 'full of grace', I was born Ann Mari Wallenberg on 4th June 1929 in Parkudden, in my mother's bedroom. My personal odyssey is about to begin.

◇

CHAPTER FOUR

◆

PARKUDDEN

Parkudden, on the Royal island of Djurgården in Stockholm.

A FEW YEARS ago I visited Parkudden after many, many years. I was out walking on Djurgården, the island near the centre of Stockholm that has been in possession of the Swedish crown for centuries. I took a detour to the eastern end of the island where Parkudden stands on the water's edge, and knocked on the front door.

The gentleman who was living there answered, and I told him that I had been born in the house. He couldn't have been more welcoming and said I could visit any time I liked, although he himself was due to move out, as the Swedish royal family were planning to use the house as a home for one of the King's daughters, Princess Madeleine, and her husband, and it was about to have a complete overhaul and restoration.

However for the moment, the house had been untouched since my mother had overseen its interior decor. Virtually nothing had been altered since I had lived there. The hallway was painted a bright scarlet red by my mother, a bold statement for anyone visiting Parkudden for the first time. In that hall had stood the grand piano my great-uncle Knut gave my parents as a wedding gift, always prominently displayed, and not just displayed but actively played, reminding me of the Mackays' love of music, and the links back to my maternal grandmother, who had studied

Left: Marc (Boy-Boy), Doie and I in the snowy driveway at Parkudden, 1930.
Right: I absolutely adored the family car.

with Liszt. That piano is still in the family: it was later passed on to my half-sister Sally and was a centrepiece of her own home at Glynde in the South Downs.

Exploring the rest of the house awoke other powerful memories, not least in the old kitchen, which still sported an open fire, just as it had when I was growing up there in the 1930s. And I could still recall the scent of the Pears Soap which my mother put in the gents: I have used it ever since.

Of course all my earliest memories are quite naturally set in Parkudden. Parkudden was my birthplace. I was born in my mother's bedroom, a lovely spacious room with a beautiful prospect looking out over the water. I later spent a lot of time in that bedroom, not least being terribly ill, in the way one was as a child, when there were no proper drugs or inoculations and one had to go through the ritual checklist of children's diseases: German measles, measles, and worst of all for me, chickenpox, those terrible spots all over that itched like mad, and which we weren't allowed to scratch: even the unpleasantly smelling lotions that were smeared over the spots did little to alleviate the intense irritation.

When I wasn't fighting chickenpox I could explore a lovely, spacious, elegant house set in its own grounds – its name means the 'park on the promontory' – with that wonderful view over Stockholm's inlets. In the 1890s the house had been created, out of an earlier residence, by Ferdinand Boberg, a leading Swedish architect of the time and a designer of anything from furniture to ceramics, all in a kind of Swedish *art nouveau* style.

Parkudden was one of five houses Boberg designed for the royal family on Djurgården, where he also lived, in a couple of villas of his own design. Parkudden was earmarked for Prince Carl, the third son of Oscar II of Sweden-Norway, and his Danish princess, Ingeborg; they and their young children lived there from 1899 to 1908. The Crown then decided to rent it out, and the first tenants were my father's aunt Ruth and her husband, Carl von Essen, who in turn made the house available for my parents in 1926.

The pattern of my life at Parkudden was, in principle, a very happy and cosseted one: there were eight servants working inside the house, plus a nursemaid for me.

Mama's influence was there throughout the house, and not just because of her bright red entrance hall. The whole house was splendidly untidy; it spilled over with books everywhere, on every subject, just as my mother spilled over with ideas. The perennial student, she attended endless courses, but also, *mens sana in corpore sano*, exercised every day, doing her callisthenics with the windows flung wide open, even when flurries of snow were coming in, and going out riding. She loved walking and skiing like anything, and to go into the city or out into the country I would be placed on a special kind of sledge while she skied behind pushing me along.

Although we children were corralled off with nannies, my mother was physically affectionate, and never distant. She was pretty good about that. The odd thing was that she was not in the least bit maternal. She thought anything to do with young children was deeply dull. A true Mackay, she was quite bored with us until we could engage in a robust debate with her.

In later years, when I had my own children, whenever she came to stay she was exactly the same. In fact, I think she got worse. One day, shortly after I had my first child Celia, my mother was staying with us, and since I had to go out, I asked her, 'Could you have Celia for the day?' Her response was, 'Of course... It doesn't matter if I don't feed her for one day, does it?' I had carried on with the family tradition of having a nanny and the children eating in the nursery, but when she visited I would get them out of the nursery. I thought it would be good for them to eat with their grandmother, but when we all sat down at the table, she would say, 'Do we have to have the children? Can't they go and eat in the nursery?'

So my primary contact on a daily basis was with my nannies. The first of these was a lovely, kind woman, but unfortunately she went mad – I don't think I had any part to play in that. When I was three or four, she locked herself in the bathroom one day, refused to come out, and had to be taken away to a lunatic asylum. She was followed by this absolute brute of nanny called Sista: she used to keep a stick in the bathroom and beat us even if we hadn't done anything, on the basis that 'You are not naughty now, but you will be'.

Into this world, like those flurries of snow, my father would blow in from time to time, always creating at the very least a squall, most often a tempest.

My memories of him are vivid, and mainly ones of terror. Marcus Wallenberg Jr was a dominant figure in every field and when he was at Parkudden a huge presence in the house, quite literally. He was very tall – six foot four. I remember once seeing him dressed as Father Christmas. I realised this was not actually Father Christmas because my father had very large feet, and distinctively shiny shoes, so as soon as I saw those enormous gleaming shoes, I knew at once it was him.

As well as his height, he was, as we know, extremely good-looking, with those chiselled, glamour-boy looks, really a beauty. He had an attractive, booming, voice; and he never stopped talking. With the combination of the looks and that voice, women would swoon. It made me feel quite sick.

There was a constant edge of conflict whenever he was around. My father could always pick a fight. He loved it. But these were never physical fights. He was not a brawler; that would have spoilt his looks... And he was strict. There were innumerable rules – many very much the things parents told children in that era, along the lines of 'Don't speak until you are spoken to' – so any breach of those sent him into a fury. I feel in retrospect that I spent a lot of time in tears when he was there.

My two brothers were also fighting, constantly. My elder brother Marc, whom we all called 'Boy-boy', was the first-born and hence the heir, with all the pressure to live up to my father's expectations, expectations which could never be matched. Peter was more precocious, and far more studious.

I loved both of them, Marc and Peter. But they were never close. This was not out of jealousy, which everyone blames, but just some deep, dark, visceral dislike – and so they continually squabbled and scrapped, rolling about wrestling on the floor, fights that my elder brother, being the physically larger, invariably won. One of my earliest memories is, aged about two, stamping my little foot, begging them to stop fighting. It felt such a shame to me, who loved them both, indiscriminately and equally, that they could never get along: what fun they could otherwise have had together.

To offset my memory, I recently found a photograph of Marc and Peter outside the garage at Parkudden, smiling away, arm in arm, with the gardener's boy who was their best friend: they obviously did have fun between the squabbles.

I don't know if their antagonism was fuelled by my father's personality. The mood in the house was very much dominated by my father because he was one of these really difficult people. My brothers' rowdy games-cum-battles often started early in the morning, about six o'clock. To begin with my father would be terrific, join in with them... and then quite suddenly his mood would change, and he'd throw them out crossly. This unpredictability was the problem. We knew he could turn just like that, like a switch being thrown, so we were always treading on eggshells.

Left to right: Peter Wallenberg, the gardener's son and Marc Wallenberg, outside the garage at Parkudden.

If my brothers were simply being boys, I was wilfully obstinate. I once refused to go and say good morning to my father, because 'I haven't said good morning to my dolls, and they haven't had breakfast yet', knowing full well I was going to get a beating, and almost proud of the fact.

My father had the same complex relationship with his own older brother Jacob as my siblings. The drive, single-mindedness and determination in my father that Doie had noticed, and probably admired early on, was in part fuelled by his ambition to beat Jacob, who was both brilliant and charmingly delightful. I often wished my uncle was my father... (Jacob, however, had his own disappointments. He had set his mind on becoming Foreign Secretary of Sweden, but he did not achieve his goal).

There were other tensions at play in Parkudden, most of which I was unaware. Some were physical: in 1931 my father had caught diphtheria, which caused him some temporary paralysis. Others were financial: the Great Depression was biting in the United States, and my mother was concerned about its impact on Mackays, who had spent heavily on the Lorimer additions to Glencruitten; their interests in the US, especially in Florida, were stretching them thinly. In the early 1930s my father was also struggling at work, for example with a shortfall for the Kreuger Group, which he oversaw for the bank, caused by the financial crisis. And as far as my life was concerned, the major tension was within my parents' marriage. These were troubled times all round.

The time I looked forward to each year were those six weeks every summer we spent in Scotland. My brothers and I loved it there. Wonderful, long evenings – not quite as long as those in Stockholm, but plenty long enough. It was a different life, like being part of a different family, as my father stayed back in Sweden. For me, it seemed as if everyone was jolly in Scotland, and gloomy in Sweden.

Every summer, as she always did from then on, Doie would go back to Glencruitten. Initially my father came along too, but it did not take long for him to stop accompanying her. Most likely he felt that he did not fit in with the Mackays' literary, musical, artistic and interests, which were very different to his.

The only downside of the visits to Glencruitten was that Sista and her particular brand of harsh discipline came too, at my father's insistence; he wanted me to have a Swedish nanny so I wouldn't forget my Swedish.

On one occasion my grandfather Alexander Mackay came over to Sweden, which was highly unusual, probably the only time he came in his life. He was always to me just a dear old man; we weren't frightened of him – but as ever, we were children to be seen and not heard: 'Run along, darling.' What was clear to me even as a child was that my mother absolutely adored her father. And my father loved him as well, which was rather extraordinary. He always said of Alexander, 'What a wonderful, upstanding man': he really admired him.

The winter trips to the Mackay property in Florida continued. My first visit there was as a six-month-old. I left Gothenburg on 7th December

1929, aboard the liner *MS Kungsholm*, a Swedish American Line vessel, accompanied by my mother, father and brothers.

In Florida, Gugsie, true to her ecclesiastical Burns heritage, was a prominent member of the local Presbyterian church. My grandmother was a terrific do-gooder. So there were parties all the time. It was, after all, the Twenties, a jolly time. She and my aunt Grace were extremely social, both involved with the Lake Alfred Woman's Club, hosting social events on the property, and opening it up to local youth groups and scout troops. There were cultural evenings, when concert pianists and chamber musicians were invited to perform. Grace, still an actress at heart, put on plays in the grounds.

Jack N. Morley, whose father, an English botanist had been hired by my grandfather to oversee the planting of the La Rochelle and manage the property, remembered those days. The Morley family lived in the extra wing of La Rochelle that had been added on to the original plans. 'The pioneer spirit prevailed in Lake Alfred in those days, when everybody's home was "open house" at all times and especially in the evenings when the younger set congregated to dance to someone's phonograph. Sometime on Thursday night when a car was available it would be loaded up with guys and gals for an evening's dancing at Proctor's Eagle Lake dance pavilion at Crystal Beach.'

I was taken to Florida on and off, not every year like the others, and it was the same when I was an adult. It depended on circumstances. My elder brother Marc, for example, ended up studying at Harvard Business School in the late 1940s and that was when he really discovered the delights of La Rochelle. The weather, compared to winter in England and Scotland, was marvellous. There were endless tennis matches on clay courts and swimming in the lake. In the boathouse down by the lake were speedboats. They were very fast, went like an absolute bomb – my father loved that, of course. We used to tear round the lakes and the connecting canals. You could go for miles.

Throughout it all Grace, or Auntie Bea as we called her (I have no idea why – another family nickname lost in the mists of time), was living

For six weeks every summer my mother returned to Glencruitten, where she could reconnect with and 'imbibe the true Mackay spirit.'

The cousins picnicking and swimming at the 'Bridge over the Atlantic' – the Clachan Bridge that connects the island of Seil with the Scottish mainland, just south of Oban. Boy-Boy, Peter and I were the constant companions of our cousins Fay and Christopher Donovan.

there pretty well permanently. She mixed *incredibly* strong Martinis as a welcoming stirrup cup. When, in the 1950s, I went with my husband, we were all drunk the minute we got in the door. In fact people who arrived at the house for the parties seemed completely drunk already. It was quite boring, actually. Although my husband thought it was rather good.

Perhaps the saddest thing about my childhood is that I can hardly remember my parents as a couple. I barely have any memories of them ever being in the same room. I do know that very early on my father moved out of their bedroom and went off to another bedroom in the house.

My mother was certainly unhappy. My cousin Susanah Mackay-James remembers letters that Doie wrote to her brother Ferrier (Susanah's grandfather) from Sweden, saying 'Why don't you answer? It's a grim time here.'

On the surface Mama tried to carry on as normal, and although she did not take part in many of my father's business activities, she did launch the ship *Laurel*, which had been built in Sweden using machinery from a Wallenberg company. She took part in some local theatre, taking a leading role in a Noël Coward comedy for the British Amateur Dramatic Society in Stockholm. She loved performing. At the age of 14 she had appeared on the bill at the Theatre Royal in Glasgow, delivering impersonations of contemporary comediennes, along with Charles Coborn (famous for singing 'The Man Who Broke The Bank At Monte Carlo').

She drove herself around: I believe she was the first woman, certainly one of the first women, to hold a driving licence in Sweden. One day she had an accident, and returned to the house to take a taxi with some house guests into Stockholm. As they drove past the scene of the accident, her friends said, 'Oh look, there's a car in the ditch.' My mother decided not to tell them she was responsible for putting it there a few hours earlier.

By the time I was only three years old, my father had left Parkudden once and for all. He was there, and the next minute he was gone. And the boys were packed off to boarding school. So for much of the time it was my mother and me and the staff at Parkudden. My mother stayed on in

Doie on the extreme left, taking part in what must have been a Spanish play with Stockholm's British Amateur Dramatic Society, 1932.

the house for three or four years, hoping that my father would come back and that they would be reconciled, in fact hoping against hope because the situation was irreversible.

That they lasted even ten years together was probably due to their shared sense of humour. A good sense of humour is always a useful glue when things start becoming unstuck in a marriage, but ultimately even that was not enough to keep them together.

The divorce terms were – I later learnt – agreed in the summer of 1934 and finalised in 1935. Under the terms of the agreement, my mother could stay at Parkudden, was given custody of us three children and an annual allowance of 50,000 kronor, with my father continuing to oversee my brothers' education, especially if Doie ever chose to leave Sweden, though not my education – not that that stopped him interfering in it.

When my father left in the autumn of 1934 he moved into a flat in the Fersenska Palatset, or Fersen Palace, in central Stockholm, just near the Wallenberg bank headquarters. He also had a new woman in his life, or at least officially she was new. Marianne was the wife of Count Carl Bernadotte: my father had met both of them attending the wedding of Count Carl's brother in New York in the winter of 1928, the trip my mother didn't feel up to because she was pregnant with me... My mother always said – especially when she was cross with me – that it was my fault that my father left because he met my stepmother on the boat going over to America.

Marianne was an aristocrat, née de Geer Friherrina af Leufsta: her family's estate was one of the largest in Uppsala County. So she was quite grand: of course she had also married the King's cousin (he was apparently completely ghastly) and consequently was very much part of royal circles – and she was Swedish, so completely *au fait* with the social world of Stockholm.

She was six years older than my father, and described by one observer as 'handsome rather than beautiful'. Unlike my mother, she loved sailing (which always made Mama extremely seasick), was a brilliant shot, and a phenomenal horsewoman. She was actually a rather remarkable woman. She had the huge family estate to look after: her father had no sons and so she was brought up like a boy and taught how to run the whole thing.

I still have an old movie my father shot that shows her in the middle of briefing her workers. Marianne is standing in a doorway with all these people coming to do obeisance in a long line, masses of them, all the women curtseying, which is what you did in Sweden in those days. Marianne was in fact terribly left-wing. My mother told me she called her 'Pinky'. But then my mother also called my husband 'Pinky' as well because she once saw him with *The Guardian* under his arm (of course he did it on purpose just to annoy her).

Marianne was a very charming woman, and she was certainly not a bad stepmother to me. When my mother remarried, she was a exemplary

My traditional Swedish outfit, often worn on family occasions, and here with our beloved sheepdog in 1935.

mother to her stepchildren, always brutally fair. Both Doie and Marianne allowed no favourites, and no one-up-manship.

Although divorce was somewhat easier to obtain in Sweden than it was in England in the 1930s, it was still frowned upon, especially within the Establishment. Marianne got divorced from Count Carl in 1935, and encountered massive disapproval as she had been part of the Royal family: it was something of scandal for the Bernadottes.

Between my parents, the Wallenbergs took my mother's side, especially once they realised that my father and Marianne had been having an affair for years. My mother had known for a long time, and confided in her friend Pamela Cobbold, but had soldiered on.

My father certainly felt the weight of their disapproval. 'It is perfectly clear,' says one biography, 'that Amalia [my grandmother] sided with her daughter-in-law'. Amalia had a finely tuned sense of decorum, but she also knew that my father had been responsible for the breakdown of the marriage. The fact that Mama stayed on at Parkudden was seen within the family as clear confirmation that it was my father's fault rather than hers that their relationship foundered.

Strangely, they got on terribly well once they were divorced: they both enjoyed their second marriages far better than their first, which possibly relaxed the old tensions. Their shared sense of humour survived, and a residual affection. At my daughter's wedding, my father came over from Sweden, and, honestly, he and my mother flirted with each other like mad. I later discovered that my father had also kept all my mother's letters, which is quite extraordinary. When you divorce someone I would have thought you put them onto the bonfire!

When my parents first separated and then divorced, I was considered too young, so there was no official explanation at all. But I do remember the moment I was sat down at the dining room table in Parkudden with my brothers by my mother. She said, 'I have got to tell you that your father and I have decided to separate and I am going to get re-married.' My younger brother broke into tears and ran out of the room. The other, Boy-Boy, simply asked, 'Who is going to keep the big car?' – that was his main concern.

This is how I learnt that my mother was re-marrying, that we would be leaving Parkudden (where despite my father's antics, I had been terribly happy), and not only that, but that my mother and I would be going to London. I don't think my mother actually told me we were leaving on a permanent basis, so I kept believing we were going back, and that this trip to London was simply an extended vacation, like going to Glencruitten for the summer. However, it would be the best part of four years before I came back to Sweden.

◇

One of the last pictures of my brothers and I all together before I went back to England: Parkudden, 1937.

◇

CHAPTER FIVE

THE HAMBROS OF LONDON

The portrait of Sir Everard Alexander Hambro, son of the bank's founder
Carl Joachim Hambro, presided over the boardroom at the bank's iconic offices
in Bishopsgate, London.

THE MAN MY mother was about to marry was Charles Hambro. Mama had been noticed by the newspapers attending a charity ball with him in December 1935, and less than a month later, on New Year's Day 1936, their marriage was announced for 15th February.

This was still only a matter of a dozen or so weeks after my parent's final divorce decree came through. Things had moved quickly for both my parents on the matrimonial front, as my father married his second wife Marianne in Copenhagen a few months later.

At my mother's second wedding, there was an extraordinary piece of visible proof of the Wallenbergs' support for my mother. My grandmother Amalia, Marcus's mother, went to my mother's second wedding but did not go to Marcus and Marianne's, which was strikingly indicative of her preference, especially as I believe it was one of the very rare times she ever went abroad. The Wallenbergs had also taken to Charles Hambro very well, because he was so charming, a bit like my father: they both bowled people over with their charm.

I, on the other hand, missed the wedding, only because I had been laid low with either measles or German measles. and was not well enough to go, even though I was meant to be a bridesmaid. Perhaps

Charles and Doie on their honeymoon, possibly visiting La Rochelle in Florida.

that initially made this new marriage less real to me, not witnessing the formal celebration.

I am not sure whether Charles Hambro had been on the scene before he and my mother became close. He and his wife Pamela had certainly been part of the group of banking 20-somethings crisscrossing and meeting up in Europe and the USA. These banking families had known each other since the late 1800s, doing business and socialising; they had many friends in common. It is possible Charles might have been to Parkudden as a guest. In any case, little children weren't really interested in the romantic side of life. We rarely saw the grown-ups; our nannies, that was our world.

My first impression of Charles Hambro was that he was very easy to get along with. He was a truly lovely man, and infinitely nicer than my own father (as I used to tell my stepfather). Like my father he was hugely tall, well over six foot, and I always remember him smiling and laughing. That was his nature, and was such a change from my own father. His voice was not particularly loud, just quiet and gentle, and he possessed extremely kind eyes. Everyone seemed to love him, although I was told by many people that he was a very tough negotiator when it came to business.

Charles Hambro and Pamela Cobbold on their wedding day in October 1919.

My future brother-in-law Andrew Gibson-Watt wrote this sketch of Charles Hambro: 'He had, in extraordinary high degree, the ability to charm people, and to make them do the exact opposite of what they wanted to do. This ability to "charm birds off trees" gave him extraordinary self-confidence.'

If my mother's family were *bona fide* Scots, the Wallenbergs pure Swedes, Charles Hambro was part of the British establishment. After Eton – where he was an outstanding bowler, who might have played for England, if war had not intervened – he had joined the Coldstream Guards. He was a genuine war hero. Aged just nineteen, he had been awarded the Military Cross after his exploits in one of the battles at Ypres, rescuing wounded comrades, taking out at least four of the enemy and capturing a clutch of prisoners. He was a fighter. Before he married my mother, he had fought, and defeated, cancer of the tongue, involving the surgical removal of chunks of his tongue, and radium needles being placed into the remnants. After weeks of agony he survived, his silver tongue intact.

The Hambros were émigré German Jews. Calmer Levy had grown up in Hamburg and moved to Copenhagen in 1778, where his requested name 'Hamborg' was changed inadvertently to 'Hambro'. His cloth business was renamed C.J. Hambro & Son in 1806 by his son Joseph, who had begun trading in money. Joseph's son Carl Joachim was sent to London in 1832 to set up a subsidiary branch of C.J Hambro & Son in 1839, and having been created a Baron, bought Milton Abbey in Dorset in the 1850s.

While Charles was on the front line in the First World War, the Hambros and the Wallenbergs were negotiating at government level. Sweden, although technically neutral, was largely pro-German, but very concerned about the threat from Russia. In 1915 a British delegation, including Charles's father Eric Hambro (a wonderfully extravagant character, who loved tiger hunting) had gone over to Sweden to meet my great-uncle Knut Wallenberg, then Minister for Foreign Affairs, to try and persuade Sweden to allow goods across to Russia. The Hambros had been bankers to the Swedish government for decades. Later the Hambros Bank helped negotiate post-war loans with Scandinavian banks.

Charles Hambro's first wife was Pamela Cobbold: the Cobbold family had been brewers in Suffolk for seven generations. Her father John Dupuis Cobbold was appointed High Sheriff of Suffolk shortly after her birth and like Charles had been to Eton, where he was a talented tennis player.

Although rooted in her home town of Ipswich, there was Scottish blood on Pamela's mother's side. Lady Evelyn was the daughter of the 7th Earl of Dunmore, head of the Scottish Clan Murray, and the grand-daughter of the Earl of Leicester. She was the first English woman to convert to Islam and make the pilgrimage to Mecca in 1933 aged 66.

Pamela spent her summers at Rannoch Lodge in Perthshire, which had been bought by her father, where she enjoyed stalking and shooting. The romance between her and Charles, who had been friends with Pamela's brother at Eton and Sandhurst, began when he visited Gannochy in

Charles Hambro in 1935

Glen Esk, an estate that the Hambros and Morgans used to rent for the summer. They married even younger than my parents: Charles was 22, Pamela was 19.

For once in my family's history, divorce was not the reason Charles was free to marry my mother. He was a widower. Pamela loved and lived life to the full. She and Charles were always going to parties and often would get into a car the following morning and drive all the way down to Dorset to go hunting. In 1931 Pamela had a riding accident: she was kicked by her hunter, and although no bones were broken, she developed septicaemia. A few months later she attended the South Dorset Hunt Point to Point Ball, and caught a bad chill in a thunderstorm. The pneumonia that developed was severe, and in the absence of antibiotics, extremely life-threatening. Her children were suffering from whooping cough and were only allowed

Doie Wallenberg in 1935

to see her through her bedroom window. Pamela never recovered, and died, aged 32, in April 1932. Charles himself, now a director of the Court of the Bank of England in addition to his responsibilities at the Hambros Bank, was only 34. He now had four young motherless children. Cynthia, the oldest, was just eleven when her mother died.

My new home was 63 New Cavendish Street in Marylebone, just off Upper Regent Street. This Georgian townhouse had been started by Robert and James Adam, and finished by John Johnson between 1775 and 1777. Just as I had visited Parkudden after decades, I returned to the Hambros' house, now called Asia House, in my eighties, and walked in because the front door was open. And again much was as I remembered it. The wonderful painted ceilings, cornices, and the elegant, grand staircase that Johnson had designed were all intact, along with the bookcases

Above: A weekend party at Rannoch Lodge. Left to right: Lady Blanche Cavendish, John (Ivan) Cobbold, Charles and Pamela Hambro and Lady Evelyn Cobbold.

Left above: Charles with his own and the Wallenberg children at Rannoch Lodge. Clockwise from top: Diana Hambro, Cynthia Hambro, Pamela Hambro, Ann Mari Wallenberg, Charles Hambro, Charlie Hambro, Peter Wallenberg, Marc Wallenberg.

Left below: Rannoch Lodge, Perthshire, the Scottish sporting estate owned by John Dupuis Cobbold, Pamela's father.

designed by Sir John Soane. And just as at Parkudden, the kitchen was instantly recognisable – the old black range where the cook used to make soufflés still there – as was my mother's bedroom, in which she had the bath sunk to floor level, and the scullery where my stepsister Pamela had her appendix whipped out just in the nick of time.

My brother-in-law Andrew Gibson-Watt, who married Pammie in the early 1950s, recalled in his own memoir these London houses. 'There was a large market in houses for temporary rent on a furnished basis, with or without servants.' London hospitals, it was felt, were places best avoided if you wanted to stay healthy, if not alive, so a surgeon would be brought in to operate 'sometimes in fact on the kitchen table'.

I was quite surprised when I arrived in this new home. Although we had staff at Parkudden, that was much more on a Russian model, where the staff were almost part of the family, and able to be very bossy. Now I was in this grand house in London with staff, all in braids. I asked my stepsisters and stepbrother where the staff slept and none of those children had ever been up there. I was horrified, because when I went to look there was just one big room full of beds with curtains round them, and I couldn't see any heating; it was freezing. In Sweden it was so different; everyone had their own room and a fire. I came back downstairs, said, 'Do you know what it is like up there?' and they were not really interested. I was rather shocked.

To come into this family, four years after Pamela's death, was difficult for everyone involved. For me, the whole situation was muddling and confusing. I was a very shy child and had loved the fact that it had just been me, my mother, and my brothers, in Parkudden, a tiny, contained little world, and now I was in this enormous household, part of an extended family of seven children. It was a huge upheaval. I missed my Swedish home immensely. Every day I would ask, 'When are we going back to Parkudden?' And my mother rarely answered me. If she ever did she said, 'We will talk about that another time', which meant never.

For Charles, who was still raw from the sudden death of his first wife, this was the house where he had lived with her, where they had had four children, with all the memories attached. My mother's role was equally daunting. She had to come in, an outsider with no connections in England because she had been in Sweden for ten years, to take over this household with two teenage girls, Cynthia and Diana (or Cynnie and Di), who slept in the same room as their father and had done so since Pamela died. So on arrival she had to turf them out, which did not make her very popular with the girls.

It is only since I have got older that I have realised how awful it must have been for my stepsisters, this new mother and child arriving in their midst. However they had plenty of opportunity to get to know my mother. She certainly saw a lot of them, especially in school holidays. Charles would take them shooting and every weekend my mother and stepfather would go to Dorset, where they had a house. When we joined them there we had much more freedom and we got away from the nannies, which was wonderful. Everyone had to get on a horse (unlike my mother, I had never been on a horse before) and ride off over the downs.

My youngest stepsister, Pamela, turned out to be a real brick. She became my best friend for the rest of her life. Just before I arrived, the poor thing had just been told she was going to have her own bedroom, for the first time in her life, and when I turned up she was told she had to forgo this.

She was extremely kind, and told me when I apologised for ruining her splendid solitude, 'Oh darling, don't be silly. Of course I'd much rather have you in my bedroom.' I am sure she didn't really, but her attitude set the tone for our friendship. I, on the other hand, remember consciously thinking, 'I don't see why either of us should put up with this. Why should we: we are both intelligent people, and I think we should both of us have our own room'.

Pamela's approach made me realise that you could get through life by being jolly nice: you didn't have to be tiresome. She was charming and made everything easy for everybody. That was a huge lesson, which I have never forgotten. You can make the world a better place if you put your mind to it, and that thought had never once occurred to me until I met this girl.

My stepbrother Charlie was a year younger than me: he was less than two years old when his mother died, so he did not remember her at all. The fact that he and I got on so well straightaway helped save the whole situation. My ruse was to let him win every board game we played. We always seemed to be indoors playing games, brought up on Monopoly as much as mother's milk.

It might have been a contrast to my parents' fighting, the issues and problems, my two brothers scrapping, but it was a complete change, a shock, a surprise, to come from a house of conflict to a family where people would be prepared to concede ground and be thoughtful about other people.

The only real problem in this move was that when I came to London I simply could not eat the food. The food at the Hambro house was a severe shock to my digestive system. I distinctly remember the first meal I was served there: a plate containing a pool of blood in which some indeterminate slice of bloody meat wallowed. In Sweden meat was always well cooked: this offering was as unpalatable to me as the runny eggs in Glencruitten. The meal was rounded off with a distinctly unappetising bowl of tapioca in milk. Compared to my diet in Sweden this was a significant downturn; food has always been very important in my life.

I was rescued by the Hambros' butler, Botwright, with whom I had luckily made friends very quickly. He sympathetically realised that I found little of what was served up to me even remotely palatable. There were frequent dinner parties held downstairs, where the food was excellent but generally never came the way of us children. Botwright would craftily sneak me some food that he had saved from those dinners, and which I accepted gratefully. Bravo for Botwright: we all need a Botwright in our lives.

We became a pretty happy family quite quickly. However, my brothers were never able to become properly part of the family in England, because they were still away at boarding school in Sweden: the Sigtuna school north of Stockholm, set up in the mid-1920s (Olof Palme, the Swedish Prime Minister assassinated in 1986, was a contemporary of my brothers).

I was sent to school in London. My stepsister Pamela remembered feeling very sorry for me, because I really did not speak very much English, and so was at something of a disadvantage when I was sent to a London school with no preparation. Glendower Prep School had been founded in the 1890s on the Fulham Road and then relocated (via Glendower Road, hence its name) to the Cromwell Road, near the V&A and the Natural History Museum. The uniform was a purple jacket and skirt – still the colours of the school 80 years on.

Charles Hambro with baby Sally, 1938.

My efforts to settle into this new life in London were occasionally disrupted by my father dragging me back to Sweden early for the summer holidays each June – summer term finished at the end of July – to be with him. He was on the look-out for a house in the country to live in with Marianne, so we would end up in some awful hotel in a seaside town. I would be there for six weeks with the usual unrelenting Swedish nanny.

In 1938 my mother and Charles had a daughter, Sally. The other Hambro children had all had the same nanny from the time before their mother died. However, with Sally's arrival, a new nanny was appointed, and as a result the nursery was far more welcoming: the walls were olive green, with an open fire, and a gramophone, where we listened to 'The Teddy Bears Picnic', along with Cynthia and Diana's latest dance music, including lots of Cole Porter and 'A Nightingale Sang In Berkeley Square' – I still love all that music.

In 1939 Cynthia and Diana had their debutante season – the photo of them in all their finery is one of my favourites. There was a glamorous dance at the house in New Cavendish Street in June that year; I remember as a child we were allowed to peek from upstairs as the guests arrived. Three months later Britain was at war with Germany.

Being presented at Court in 1936 by Lady Hambro, (Doie's new
mother-in-law), were left to right: Mrs Richard Hambro, Cynthia Hambro,
Lady Hambro, Doie, Charles and Diana Hambro.

CHAPTER SIX

◇

RETURN TO STOCKHOLM

Stockholm, 1939.

The day war was announced I was in the Hambros' house in Dorset: they had put me into a little local school I used to bicycle to every day. It was the most lovely late summer's day, gorgeous weather. I came in and was told we were at war. I listened to a repeat of the announcement during the evening news on the wireless. I have a photograph in my head of the sitting room with a whole lot of people in it, people we did not often see, including my stepfather Charles's sister and even his mother (rather a splendid woman: she had breakfast in bed and smoked cigars).

Quite soon after the start of the war, I found myself heading back to Sweden, because my father insisted I should return. He said that he did not want me 'to be invaded by the Germans. I don't want my daughter to be in a war, thank you very much, she is better off with me'. And my mother couldn't really say no to that, because she was considering my safety. She was a terribly loyal person and would do whatever was best for her children. Any personal issue would be put out of the window. This of course meant my father was going to be in charge of the next phase of my life, which was not by any means my idea of wonderful.

When I was told that I might go back to Sweden – even though this was something I had been warned might happen as war looked more and

Gothenburg port, 1939.

more likely – I was plunged into depression, because I knew the heavy
hand of my father was going to come into play. In addition, by then I
had become tremendous friends with all the Hambro children; we were
getting on really well.

When I had arrived in London I had gone through all that business
of wanting to stay in Sweden. Now I wanted to stay in London and was
horrified at the prospect of being split up from my new best friend Pamela.
It was the kind of thing that could really upset children.

The whole thing was a huge wrench. My stepsister Pammie said that
she had a strong impression that having formed this relationship with me
she might well never see me again – that I would vanish without trace.

And so I went back to Sweden, a day and a half by boat to Gothenburg
with my ferocious nanny, and, believe it or not, my stepbrother Charlie.

The Fersen Palace, seen on the left of the picture, was sombre and forbidding.
Marcus Wallenberg occupied one of the top floors.

He was uprooted from London and dispatched to Stockholm alongside me, poor thing, to keep me company. When they told us this, he complained bitterly and rightly, 'I don't know why I am going'. Maybe everyone thought they were being kind because we were such great friends. Whatever the reason, we were all horrendously sick on the boat across; the North Sea was always terribly rough. Then once we reached Gothenburg, we had to endure seven hours on the train to Stockholm.

There we were installed in my father's apartment in the Fersen Palace. This building, if you had an architectural bent and were not an exhausted, recently seasick child, was impressive. It had originally been designed in the 1630s as the Admiralty House, close to the Swedish Navy's then principal base.

When the Navy (and Admiralty House) relocated in the 1650s, Queen Christina decided that the building, immediately across the water from the Royal Palace, should be converted into residential accommodation, eventually, via various inheritances, arriving in the family of the von Fersens, who modernised it and reconstructed the palace. Count Axel von Fersen was extremely close to Marie-Antoinette (they were rumoured to be lovers) and tried to save her after the execution of Louis XVI. He went back to Sweden where he was killed by a lynch mob in 1810 because he was suspected of involvement in the overthrow of King Gustavus IV the year before – all very melodramatic.

When the von Fersen dynasty collapsed, the palace was re-built a third time, in the 1880s, with multiple apartments for rent. My father had one of the top floors, with this marvellous, shallow, marble staircase, so that a horse could be ridden to the top of the building: everything had to be carried up those stairs.

The building itself was imbued with the tragic story of the von Fersens, and to me appeared always very dark and gloomy. I was constantly being thrown out into a dreary roof garden on top of the building. I never remember a single shaft of sunlight in the place, just gloom, gloom, gloom. Being handed a sandwich with a sort of liver pâté – that was almost the only bright spark.

This whole mood was exacerbated by a governess who boxed my ears, which was jolly painful: I can tell you she had a pretty good pair of knuckles. I certainly didn't like her. I always say she was ghastly but it turns out she was very nice; it was just me who thought she was ghastly. She thought she was rather smart because she was lady-in-waiting to one of the royal family.

On the other hand, as I seemed to do in every place I lived, I loved the cook, and the rest of the staff were wonderful; they were terribly sorry for me in this awful mess. As well as my father and stepmother, my stepsister Catharina, Marianne's daughter, who was three years older than me, was occasionally there. She added a sunny shaft of fun, but unfortunately she was not there very often.

Of course. moving back to Stockholm meant going to another school: having just got my English up to speed I was straight back into Swedish mode. But I was lucky. Poor Charlie was sent off to the same boarding school as my brothers, where he was placed in a room with the son of the German ambassador. They probably thought it was character-forming. He used to come back black and blue..

Our family's political landscape at the time was complicated. My uncle Jacob was very engaged with Germany; in fact, he tried to arrange a coup, to simply not have the war at all.

My father was also always away and negotiating for the government: he had met Hermann Göring in 1938, when Göring was Minister of Economics, and later as part of wartime trade negotiations with Britain was sent to a meeting with Winston Churchill. The British were concerned about the danger of pushing Sweden towards the Nazis, particularly because Sweden was a vital source of iron ore. Just as Sweden had been neutral but pro-Germany in the First World War, there were a lot of pro-Germans at the start of the Second. The Russians were still the bad boys in my childhood. My nanny was always telling me, 'The Russians are coming': that was the great fear.

My father was a great friend of the British Ambassador to Sweden, Victor (later Sir Victor) Mallet, as they had known each other long before the war. Victor Mallet's mother had been a Maid of Honour to Queen Victoria – and he was her godson. He and Marcus saw each other all the time and of course communicated about the situation endlessly.

Victor Mallet, apart from his royal connections, was an old school diplomat – Winchester and Balliol, followed by stints in Tehran (then in Persia), Brussels and Washington. When he had joined the Diplomatic Service just after the War it had recently been amalgamated with the

My father's study, scene of many a confrontation.

Foreign Office: there was even a meagre salary available, since beforehand it had been assumed that diplomats would be able to live off a private income.

Sir Victor wrote an (unpublished) memoir, in which he captures something of those times. Communications were based on cypher telegrams. 'This was already considered a sad climb-down from the good old Victorian days when an Ambassador would act first and report afterwards.'. The Embassies – actually quite few in number; most were Legations – were 'like grand family parties. The big Embassies were provided with silver, some of which was very magnificent. When I was appointed to Stockholm I was informed that this post had just been provided with silver. As an afterthought, a week later, I was told that the silver did not include knives, as apparently the Treasury could not run to them.' He was advised he

Above and opposite: My stepmother, Marianne Wallenberg and my father,
Marcus, set for a day's sailing with a group of friends.

would have to go out and buy the requisite number of knives. 'I may have been the last victim of this form of lunacy.'

When he arrived in Stockholm in early 1940, a few months after war had been declared, he found Sweden a neutral country, 'but very much closer to immediate events than in the America of the Neutrality Act period. In the autumn there had been negotiated an Anglo-Swedish War Trade Agreement by 'three of the shrewdest men in Sweden, all three known to be good friends of our country', including my father. These three wise men were of the view that Britain had significantly over-estimated its own strength and under-estimated that of the Germans. The issue of ball-bearings, vital for industrial (and arms) manufacture, was a bone of contention. Sweden had the requisite iron ore, but wanted to maintain trade with Germany, whose Ruhr coalfields possessed the coal much needed by Sweden.

Outside the stress of diplomacy, Victor Mallet enjoyed the social life of Stockholm. He occasionally played King Gustav V – who was anti-Nazi, even though his wife was German – at the Royal Lawn Tennis Club, 'a somewhat alarming proceeding, as he always had the best player, generally of Davis Cup rank, as his partner'.

I was quite proud of my father because he seemed to be doing 'very important' things. However, I hardly ever saw him precisely because he was off negotiating with the British on behalf of the Swedish government, and was constantly over in London, where he took up residence at the Savoy Hotel. He and the other Swedish negotiators managed to drink up much of the Savoy's stock of vintage claret.

And unbeknownst to me, my stepfather Charles was – as well as his work for the Bank of England and the Hambros Bank – now installed in the upper echelons of what would become the Special Operations Executive.

In April 1940, the Germans walked into Denmark and then Norway. On the evening of 8th April, Ambassador Mallet was at dinner in Gothenburg with the British Consul there and the shipping magnate Gunnar Carlsson, when they were informed that the German fleet was passing through the Skagerrak, the strait between Denmark, Norway

German troops invade Norway in April 1940. In spite of Sweden's neutrality, the Wehrmacht's presence right on the border throughout the duration of the war, and the free movement of Nazi troops throughout Scandinavia, created an atmosphere of deep uncertainty and fear.

and Sweden. They confidently expected the Royal Navy would see off this irritating incursion: next morning they heard that the Germans had occupied Denmark and captured ports in Norway.

It seemed such a surprise. Up until that point the war had seemed to be something happening to other people. Sweden was absolutely neutral – a British intelligence report said, 'Sweden may be summed up as a mixture of terror and shame, possibly coupled with a certain amount of satisfaction that the war has so far passed her by' – but people started panicking.

My stepmother Marianne, along with most Swedes, was convinced the Germans were about to arrive any minute. Stockholm was in a complete state of panic. She told my brothers, 'When you see the planes in the sky, get on your bikes and hide in the basement at my friend's house until we come and find you'. Marianne had a plan in place, that she and her daughter were going into the woods to ride north. And I rather pathetically asked, 'What is going to happen to me?' She said, 'Oh, you will have to stay here and wait for your father'.

Off they went, leaving me behind. That has stuck in my mind for ever. A bad moment, one of my worst. The flat was more depressing than ever. Everything seemed dark and oppressive. The huge reception rooms were even more ominously gloomy than ever.

And then a miracle took place. My mother arrived at the Fersen Palace quite unexpectedly in April 1940. I had been writing letters to her all the time I was in Sweden but she had never written back.

The doorbell of the flat rang. I went to answer it, opened the door, and there was my mother. Just like that, no forewarning: one of the golden memories in my life, this freedom figure who appeared unannounced, and I thought to myself, 'Now I can get out', selfishly thinking of myself. It was wonderful.

She and Charles had been in Stockholm for a few days, living in a small hotel nearby. Their arrival was recounted by Ambassador Victor Mallet who wrote that in the immediate aftermath of the German occupation of Denmark and Norway, 'before long there arrived Mr and Mrs Charles Hambro, who had been in Oslo when the Germans landed. He was on an official mission from the Ministry of Economic Warfare and his wife had been intending to come to Stockholm to see some of her Wallenberg children.' So it was not in fact a miracle, but for me it was as close as I ever came to one.

I was only allowed to visit my stepfather in their hotel. He was keeping his head down on top-secret SOE business (as it turned out, setting up the Swedish end of the operation). He was technically based at a Legation Office, having been appointed a naval attaché by the Ambassador to gain diplomatic immunity, lending money to the president of the Norwegian parliament who had taken refuge in Stockholm, bizarrely also called Charles Hambro.

They had to move out because Charles was told he was on a Nazi blacklist, and the hotel was not safe. They ended up talking in the bath-

The only surviving picture of beloved Hedge End Cottage in Dorset, used by the Hambro family throughout the war. Charles Hambro is holding a scarce bottle of wine, and the garden has been 'dug for Britain.'

room with all the taps on. They were told not to drink the water because it might be poisoned. It was a horrible feeling. There was a desperate air throughout the city. The place was a hotbed of intrigue, crawling with rumours and spies: I was always being followed back from school. Yet at the same time, we carried on with our lives, going to school, skating every day – I honestly don't know how we managed, it was so peculiar.

As the hotel became increasingly unsafe, with dubious people wandering in and out, Charles and my mother moved into a flat belonging to my father's sister: she told them, 'Have it for as long as you want it'. That didn't please my father one bit. He and Charles were like alpha males prowling around each other, a lot of male pride at stake, regardless of the wartime situation. Although my father and Charles had spent time together and socialised, it was no longer – if it had ever been – through choice. My father was a very difficult man, and was not at all popular with either the Brits or the Swedes, quite honestly, but he was very, very influential, so it was worth being a friend of his. I think that essentially they truly disliked each other, and of course both of them were or had been married to my mother...

Yet my father couldn't argue as he was never at home, and the offer by his sister of the use of her flat was proof yet again that the Wallenbergs adored my mother. However, I can remember my stepbrother saying to his father, 'I am not going to go back to that silly Swedish school, unless you sort out my life so that we are all going to join up again and make things the way it was when we were all happy': some lovely childish statement like that.

As things got worse, the British Embassy told my mother and Charles that they really had to get out of the country. The British view was that to get Sweden into the war they had to reclaim Norway. There was a mission by Admiral Evans to see King Haakon of Norway, who was in hiding. The Admiral's plan was to cross the border in full uniform, in a white car, with a chauffeur. But the plan to capture Trondheim ended in disaster.

The situation was becoming untenable. So they hatched a plan for them, with me, to flee Sweden.

Mama went into the Wallenberg bank to tell my father. My father was horrified by the news, but legally could not stop her. Christiana Mallet, the Ambassador's wife, happened to be walking past the bank just as my mother came down the steps, looking like a ghost. She was taken off for a stiff brandy in the Grand Hotel.

So then I had to endure a ghastly interview with my father in his flat, when he realised I was going to leave. To be perfectly honest, it felt more like an interrogation.

Picture this huge, dark room, with a vast ceiling high out of sight. He put me in a chair and turned a light on my face just like the movies. The rest of the room was dark, so I couldn't see him. He gave me a real grilling, accused me of treachery – 'You are being a traitor to your country.' I was ten years old. It went on and on and on, for a very long time, I was reduced to tears. 'How can you do this, leave your family?' He demanded I change my mind and stay, and then when I refused, said, 'I won't be able to help you', menacingly.

At the end of the interview, with me snivelling, he told me to go to bed. He was never very good with tears or anything like that. For many years afterwards I wondered how he could have thought I was being treacherous, in what way a traitor. From that moment on the experience coloured my view of my father.

However, I can now see, in a way, why he felt he had to do it. He was jealous of my stepfather – he knew I was very fond of him. And from his point of view, this plan to leave Sweden really was an uncertain step in the dark that might take his daughter out of his life forever.

◇

◇

CHAPTER SEVEN

LOST IN TRANSIT: MOSCOW AND BUCHAREST

Bucharest in 1940.

The situation in Stockholm in the Spring of 1940 was complex, febrile, strange... and that was just within my own family. Around us swirled a heady mix of rumours, half-heard reports and speculation, fake news before it had a name.

Sweden stayed resolutely neutral, even if some in Britain saw the country as pro-German. Certainly there were businessmen and women and aristocrats with close ties to Germany, but Victor Mallet, the British Ambassador, was convinced that the middle and working classes were strongly anti-Nazi.

As the newly appointed head of what would become the Special Operations Executive's Scandinavian arm, my stepfather Charles Hambro was already deep within the murky world of espionage and secret intelligence. He had been sent to Sweden, because the precursor of the SOE, known as Section D, had had, as one of the histories of the SOE puts it, 'an organisation in Sweden which was blown in April 1940, having accomplished little'.

Charles was something of an outsider, since he was essentially a banking executive, and neither a military man or an intelligence veteran. One assessment of Charles's time in SOE (an organisation he became head of by the end of 1940) was that he 'lived by bluff and charm'. He obviously did it very well.

There were various characters drifting in and out of the British Embassy and our Stockholm flat – each could have been deftly drawn in a John le Carré novel. In this supposedly neutral country, they all seemed to have fingers in any number of mysterious pies.

As well as the Ambassador Victor Mallet, there was man called Denham in the British Embassy. He was full of ideas, mainly focused around the issue of ball bearings. A Swedish company, SKF, was a world leader in ball bearing manufacture, which was vital to the smooth running of machines and especially the war machine, on both sides. This particular issue occupied a lot of British think time.

There was also Gubbins, Major-General Colin Gubbins – later Sir Colin – who became Charles's deputy at the SOE, a completely different personality to my stepfather: a typical army type.

From my perspective it all seemed terribly amateurish in a way: every one involved, whether British, Swedish or German, seemed to have known each other in their pre-war social lives, had probably been to a night club or played tennis together at some point.

The Ambassador, Victor Mallet, remembered that at this time, when not many Swedish friends cared to be seen in his company, fearing reprisals later on if and when Germany took over Sweden, 'we got to appreciate very specially the friendship of Marc Wallenberg and his family.' In the evenings at the Saltsjöbaden hotel, 'we made use of the splendid tennis courts. Marc Wallenberg often came down to play with us and gave us an excellent dinner in the public restaurant attached to the hotel. Victor and my father made the most of it, by 'appearing to be quite unconcerned and cheerful about the outcome of the war' towards any Germans or 'doubtful' Swedes also dining there.

The same kind of jolly japes, boy scout, gung ho attitude was applied to the problem of how my mother, my stepfather and I could all get out of Sweden. I still do not know if this was because it was imperative that Charles left, since he was on a Nazi deathlist and with the prospect of a German invasion could not be allowed to be at risk. Or whether in addition my mother and I might be vulnerable pawns, who could have been captured and traded for Charles. I am sure we could have quite easily been hidden all through the war, but I don't think they dared risk it.

Whatever the reasoning, my overriding impression was that it was all a game, a typical British game, rather naughty. Everyone seemed to be thoroughly enjoying it, so they were always laughing about something, even though the state of the nation, and our lives, were at stake. It was difficult to believe how deadly serious it all was.

The first idea was that we would be lent my Swedish uncle Jacob's motor car, slapping some CD plates on it, and that my mother and I would drive north out into the forests. There was, so one rumour had it, a secret headquarters for the Swedish government somewhere out there.

The car was a two-seater but had a large boot into which, so the plan went, we would load camping equipment. This in itself was not a great idea as my mother absolutely hated camping. But nonetheless we had to traipse round Stockholm trying to buy tents, billycans, sleeping bags. Every day we were amassing saucepans and suitable accessories.

Unlike the naive William Boot in *Scoop*, there was no handy Army & Navy Store where we could head off to to acquire the necessary and put it all on account. Swedes were sailors, not campers, so it took us a while and many shopping expeditions to pile up the kit.

That plan never saw the light of day. What a waste of money. Somewhere there must still be a cache of camping equipment in some basement in Stockholm. I was much more practical than my mother. I knew the whole idea was impossible. I remember saying, 'What about petrol, Mama? There aren't any shops up there, where are we going to get petrol?' And she would airily say, 'Oh, that will all be fine.' I admired my mother enormously: I thought she was so brave, but she was foolhardy.

I always wanted to know about things. The adults tried to fob me off but they couldn't, because I wanted to know why it was like that, why it was such a mess.

The odd thing was we all went along with it. People complain so much nowadays. Then you didn't complain. You kept quiet. And actually as a child I don't think I minded because we realised that not only was it important but there was a certain amount of excitement involved. It felt like we were on a mission. It was made exciting, 'We've got to "escape"', but nonetheless I was terribly worried. I knew it was all bad.

In any case, I definitely did not want to be left behind, which was the alternative. I think I was once asked if I wanted to stay behind in Sweden but that was never an option I wanted to consider after the interview with my father. He had treated me so badly that day that I became a little less Swedish, I'm afraid. My loyalties were always confused, my allegiances divided. In England I was seen as a Swede and in Sweden as a Brit, but for the moment the balance had tilted.

The people who were really not enjoying this whole process in any way were my brothers, who were stuck at boarding school. They were just praying that they might get away. They wanted to do that more than anything, but they were never included in any plans. That is a tragic part of our family history because they never got away, and I know they felt that terribly from then on, because they thought everyone had abandoned them, which is exactly what happened. My brother-in-law Andrew Gibson-Watt believed that the reason Marc and Peter were left behind was because 'they would have dynastic business responsibilities in Sweden'.

New plans were formulated. One scheme involved a destroyer coming to the north of Sweden to pick up the embassy staff, including my stepfather and mother but not the children. My mother said she would stay with us and not go with my stepfather. So that idea was canned.

Then we were going to leave Sweden by plane. This time there were no tents involved, no billycans, and hardly any luggage, only one small suitcase each. Just before we were due to leave I went down with a raging flu or something similar, and was running a temperature of 102°F. My mother was being advised by everyone not to take me with her, because I was ill, but luckily one of the doctors whom my mother had known when she was at Parkudden, tugged at her arm and said, 'Take Ann Mari.'...

And so the journey began... to where, no one had yet bothered to inform me. The three us – Mama, Charles and I – clambered into a small, bright orange aeroplane, with some other passengers, mainly

Scandinavian, although we were never introduced, and set off flying very low, almost at ground level, and terribly slowly. I was sick as a dog. The whole aeroplane was sick.

After crossing some sea, we landed to refuel, and I found we were in Russia, in a town called Velikiye Luki somewhere on the other side of the Baltic. My overriding memories of that first stop are appalling lavatories, truly appalling, and only something disgusting to eat. That was a foretaste, a fore-odour maybe, of things to come.

We landed near Moscow, and at the airport we found ourselves incarcerated, placed in a room with a high-up window and bars on it. If I wanted to go to the loo a guard had to come too. Apparently there had been a dreadful mix-up with the papers. We had got the wrong day. It was a Wednesday but not the right date or something like that. Again it seemed so amateurish, a bureaucratic blunder, or maybe it was because the Russians were using the Gregorian calendar.

Whatever the reason the Russians had no sense of humour about the mix-up. My mother was always trying to make a joke, and it fell flat every time. It wasn't much fun. That is the sort of thing children hate; they can't bear that sort of mistake, a *grown-up* mistake. We were stuck in this room, virtually a cell, for hours while the problem was resolved. One is so impatient at the age of ten. I am sure I was thoroughly tiresome.

Charles was working hard to find a way through the bureaucracy. He kept asking to be allowed to ring the British Embassy but they refused for a long time. Eventually the discrepancy with the documents was sorted out and we went to a British Embassy flat. As we were getting ready to have dinner, I was sitting in the kitchen with the cook. She immediately started saying, in broken English, 'I want you to listen intently to what your parents are talking about, and then tell me what they are saying.' She was a daunting woman. I remember thinking, 'This can't be right' and so mumbled something back. Later she grabbed me and said, 'Have you heard anything?' When I said, 'No, nothing interesting at all.' I instinctively knew it was wrong. But it made me nervous.

We stayed in Moscow for a week or so, and went sightseeing every day.

Doie, smiling bravely for the camera, during the passport checks in Kiev.

As we walked around I had the impression that we were being followed everywhere, not just by the two obvious guards we had been allocated but by the entire population of Russia, roaming the streets with a retinue of followers, who were so very, very poor: my clothes were continually being touched. We were certainly extremely well dressed for travellers.

On one occasion we went into a church, and my mother went up to the guards, snatched the cigarettes out of their mouths, and told them not to smoke in church – in English, which of course they did not understand. And she got away with it. Charles was quite worried about that. He said, 'You'll have us in the gulag any minute if you go on like this'.

Eventually we got onto a train, heading for Romania, which, under its King Carol II, was officially neutral, although there were powerful fascist forces in the country urging to government to side with the Nazis. The train journey took several days, trundling across a seemingly endless plateau.

Stalin's genocide trains, a terrible memory that has remained with me to this day.

Our fellow passengers included a number of Norwegians who were also escaping. They became very popular with us because they had lots of food. We had none, and had been eating off station platforms, all pretty revolting fare.

Although there was no food, we were travelling in some version of luxury. We were in one of the Tsar's old carriages, with quite a few remaining trappings, including comfortable lavatories. The awful thing was that every time we stopped, there was a surge of people trying to get on the train and being beaten back with whips, not sticks but whips, which really horrified me as a child. We were locked in to our carriage, presumably to stop people getting in rather than to prevent us getting out. Even so my mother took me down to see the third-class carriage; she wanted me to see that not everyone was travelling like us.

Along the way, we stopped at one station, probably in the Ukraine, possibly in Kiev. We had been placed in a siding, which worried Charles. A lot of guards came into the carriage and started checking our passports. My mother and I got out of the carriage, and walking around the sidings heard this moaning, groaning noise coming from another train. We thought there might be some cattle in there.

We walked towards it and saw human fingers poking through the slats of some freight cars. People had been crammed in there. No water, no food. My mother knew all about Stalin herding the peasants into foul camps, all that purging that was going on; they were moving huge blocks of people. Russia was a continuous moving train of humanity.

She said we must go and look, and as we got closer there was this overpowering, terrible smell of human odour. We never got rid of the stench: when, later on, we opened our suitcase the smell had got in even though our clothes were clean. To this day I have never got rid of the memory of that smell.

We reached Bucharest – where the atmosphere felt like true freedom. The lights were on, and we all had a brief moment of cheer.

Once again we headed for the British Embassy. Through his banking connections, my stepfather knew the ambassador, who had the wonderful

The British Ambassador, Sir Reginald Hoare's residence in Bucharest.

The formal drawing room and dining room at the Embassy,
where children were not welcome.

title Envoy Extraordinary and Minister Plenipotentiary, Sir Reginald Hoare, whose family's private bank, C. Hoare & Co. dated from the 17th century.

At the time Romania was relatively calm, at least on the surface: Sir Reginald Hoare's sister Constance had visited her brother in Bucharest recently and reported that the people seemed 'cheerful and confident; the government firm; there was a strong pro-Ally feeling'.

One other Bucharest resident was Olivia Manning, who had moved there when her husband Reggie Smith, a lecturer with the British Council, was posted to the Romanian capital. She was more aware of the tensions at play in the city. On the one hand, Bucharest ('the Paris of the East') was promoting itself in a 1940 documentary as a city 'with modern boulevards, well-groomed streets and parks, wrapped in an air of normality, animated by the presence of actors, merchants and gypsy flower girls.' She described it instead as 'a strange half-Oriental capital... primitive, bugridden and brutal.'

Romania was still a neutral country, which meant that just as in Lisbon, Casablanca, or Stockholm for that matter, intrigue was rife. The Athénée Palace hotel was the hub, where Gestapo agents, British intelligence officers and foreign press correspondents stirred up rumours, and analysed the growing strength of pro-Fascist movements in the country. Sir Reginald Hoare had been sent to Bucharest to encourage interest in the Little Entente, an alliance promoted by France of Romania with Czechoslovakia and Yugoslavia, but it had collapsed just before the war – and Romania sided with the Axis powers in November 1940, six months after our arrival.

The embassy was very grand, with footmen standing behind the chairs in the huge dining room. They also had a very old English nanny who had brought up all their children. Sir Reginald did not like children, and I was promptly dispatched into the kitchen with the cook.

Consequently I did not see much of Sir Reginald, but many people believe he was the model for Sir Montagu, the British minister in Olivia Manning's *Balkan Trilogy*. 'Sir Montagu was standing in the middle of the room, leaning on his stick. His face, dark, handsome and witty, with thick folds of skin on either side of a heavy mouth, was like the face of some distinguished old actor.'

I was delighted to have been sent to the kitchen because the atmosphere in the dining room was rather strained. And then I couldn't believe it, as this ancient nanny had the cheek to tell me to go to bed at six o'clock because I was ten years old. It was such an affront. I can feel it even now. I had just been travelling halfway across Europe and been up to God know's what time. So I refused. 'I am not going to bed at six o'clock, sorry.' She was furious. That was pretty funny.

We were not in Bucharest very long, maybe just the one night; there was a great rush to press on. The ambassador's wife, Lucy, Lady Hoare – née Cavendish-Bentinck – who in comparison to her husband was very sweet, decided to come with us, and I was asked, or told, to carry her hatbox for miles. There was no taxi, which I thought was odd because the Hoares were so grand.

The hatbox was enormous, and weighed a ton; it certainly had more than a few hats in it – tins of food, I think. I got this terrible stitch (do children have stitches any more?). I can remember being shouted at as I lagged behind lugging this hatbox along, 'Hurry up, hurry up!' We were late for the train, which must have been held for us. (I later lost the hatbox somewhere along the way, God knows what was actually in it).

It was time for more of my incessant questions? 'Yes, we're going on a train, darling.' 'But where? And why?' I was terribly inquisitive, but nobody seemed to have any answers. I knew that no one really knew, because they said so out loud. Even though Charles was decisive by nature, and always the voice of authority throughout, he could not, or chose not to, tell me where we were going. So once again we headed off, on another train, into another void.

The writer Veronica Horwell, in a review of Olivia Manning's *Balkan Trilogy*, captures our journey almost perfectly, writing about the main character Harriet Pringle travelling through Romania: 'Harriet glimpses the unexplained through the window, bright eyes of beasts racing through the Romanian forest by the trackside. "Anything can happen now," she thinks.

'This is the travel of dismay – dismay means being divested of power or ability. There's no thrill in this journeying. Too much is being ventured, always to be lost in transit. Manning's great insight is that journeys happen moment by moment, so a minute of relief and security can override an hour of fear, until the next mishap.'

Out of Bucharest station we trundled, on to that next mishap.

Swedish citizens had been warned to pack up at a moment's notice: delivery cart, Stockholm 1940.

CHAPTER EIGHT

◇

FLEEING THE WAR: MILAN AND PARIS

Crowds waiting for the trains at Milan station, 1940.

For decades the essential handbooks for British travellers were the range of *Bradshaw's Guides* based around the rail networks, first published in the 1840s. For those venturing to Europe and beyond, a vital part of the packing list was *Bradshaw's Continental Railway & Hotel Guide*, combining highly detailed railway timetables, including the most far-flung and minor branch lines, alongside information about steamers on the Nile, Rhine, Danube and the Swiss Lakes, 'Diligence and Motor Services', ferries and passenger boats and advertisements for hotels across Europe.

The edition for late 1938 is still blithely oblivious to impending conflict: the ads on the inside front cover are for 'Freudenstadt calling! Germany's sun trap in the Black Forest' and 'Ems, the historic spa – world-renowned cures against Catarrhs and Asthma'. The bookmark is for the Dover-Dunkerque ferry: 'every night, Sunday included'. There is also a plug for British Airways (which shortly afterwards merged with Imperial Airways to create BOAC; three decades later the name British Airways was revived). It promised to make 'your journey a tonic, not a tussle'...

I do not remember whether Charles Hambro carried a copy of *Bradshaw's* with us on our whirlwind tour of Europe – maybe in any case the neatly chronicled train timetables had already been completely de-railed – but the map it includes shows that after landing in Velikiye

Luki we had probably travelled east to Moscow via Smolensk, and then headed along a southerly route through Kursk and Kiev to Odessa, before trundling down to Bucharest.

For the next leg of our journey we were travelling west, across Yugoslavia to Trieste and Northern Italy: yet more stations, more scrabbling for food, more uncertainty. In due course we arrived in Milan.

This felt like some kind of normality; at least we now recognised the place names. But what we had not expected was the vehement anti-British attitude. This was May 1940: Mussolini had hesitated how to react at the outbreak of war and was still making his mind up. General Wavell, who was Commander-in-Chief Middle East, came up with a powerful image, describing *Il Duce*'s dilemma: 'I think he must do something. If he cannot make a graceful dive, he will at least have to jump in somehow; he can hardly put on his dressing-gown and walk down the stairs again.' Italy, in particular the northern cities, was in a warlike trance.

When we arrived in Milan, the locals, hearing our English voices, started at best booing us, at worst spitting on us. My mother had the perfect riposte. She was fluent in German, because she had always had German governesses: my grandmother wanting to show off about her mother having being taught by Liszt in one of the best colleges in Munich.

Mama and her siblings all spoke German well. One of her sisters had done a lot of travelling in Europe in the 1930s, and had sent home a postcard of Hitler, with the message, 'We thought you would find this card very amusing'. My stepsisters had also been to Germany in the couple of years leading up to wartime.

So Mama quickly started speaking very loudly in German; we went into a hotel to get lunch and she took over, addressing the waiter in German all the time. As soon as she started talking German, everyone had their arms around her... It was a brilliant move to counter an extremely tricky moment. One more day and I am convinced we would all have been interred. This simply added to my state of fear. I had pretty much been terrified the entire way from Stockholm, feeling this hidden, unsettling sense of permanent panic which permeated all of us.

Now we turned north, crossing the border into France and up the Rhône valley towards Paris. The Luftwaffe was bombing the train the entire way, while we were trundling along. That was extremely frightening because we could hear the planes overhead. The attacks actually made Mama much calmer, because she had to be calm for me. I noticed the change in her voice. It was panicky to start with, and then she was able to control it.

If there was damage to any part of the exceedingly long train, we screeched to a halt, everyone got out and the carriage that had been hit was uncoupled and left behind. Then it was all over, and those of us who could all crammed back on. Others were simply left behind to fend for themselves: I always wonder what happened to them.

Each stop was another in an extraordinary series of events. By now, everything seemed normal, although a different kind of normal. We had no idea of what was going on it the rest of Europe, or how the war was progressing. We were locked in this bubble moving along the rails, trying to reach Paris and from there, hopefully, home. One of most amazing things about this journey is how close and how often we were to being killed at any moment.

We were by now a small group of refugees, some of whom we had been with ever since Russia. At each stop new passengers joined the train, including a few Germans who'd turned their coats.

Food remained a problem, a terrible worry. There was no food available for sale on the train. We had to scrounge for something to eat, buying it off the platform. The vendors got there pretty fast, hovering all the time. Thank goodness they did, because otherwise we would not have got anything. Any money, any currency would do at this point. Before the war, there had been all the endless *bureaux de change*, the traveller's cheques, the fun of the different notes and coins. Now anything went.

I was oblivious to what happened with the money, and the passports. Charles was in charge. We must all have been travelling on British passports, though maybe he had some kind of diplomatic passport which gave us a veneer of protection, and to ease things at certain border controls.

Aerial warfare: the Luftwaffe attack railway lines in France, May 1940.

What I realise now is that nobody at home, either in England or Sweden, had a clue where we were or whether we were still alive – my poor brothers, and Charlie, stuck in Sweden had no news. How shocking! How could I disappear? I was too fat... Maybe from the British Embassies we stayed at Charles had been able to send some kind of message back home.

But to all intents and purposes we were floating along like jetsam on a tide of warlike chaos, trying to get to Paris before the Germans occupied it – and probably not even aware that was a possibility. By the time we were close to the French capital, in May 1940, the Germans were well on the way to defeating the Allied forces in France. The evacuation of Dunkirk was imminent.

Despite the bombing raids, we made it to Paris, where we discovered that in principle there was no entry for children into Paris, which was a bit awkward for us as we arrived on this train. Since the start of the war there had been a mass evacuation of children during their Phoney War (*La drôle de guerre*), because everyone sensed that Paris was about to fall.

The American press tracking the Nazi's inexorable march
on France, May 1940.

Most were parcelled off to relatives in rural villages. As far as I could see there was not one single child except me in Paris at that moment.

Without children, Paris was full of women – the men were all fighting as usual: their favourite occupation, I always say – and every single woman in the city, it seemed, came up and shouted at my mother, 'You've got a child in Paris, you know it's not allowed. It's against the law now. You have got to take your child away and out'. My mother, as was her nature, answered back, 'Well, I can't help it, it's not my fault', or something like that. 'I am just doing what I am told.'

And then bless her, she turned to me and said, 'We are in Paris, and wouldn't you like to go up the Eiffel Tower, darling?' Of course! So off we went to the top of the Eiffel Tower in the midst of all this drama. Where yet again people came up all the time, saying 'What on earth are you doing with a child in Paris. The Germans are coming?' 'Just going up the Eiffel Tower, doing a bit of sightseeing!'

Perhaps she was trying to normalise things for me, after the train journey where everyone had been on edge. Many other people would have given in, or gone for a lie down in a darkened room, but Mama was made of stern stuff.

We must have eaten in Paris, probably the last decent restaurant going. Then it was back to what we hoped would be the final train, from Paris St-Lazare out to the port of Le Havre. What we had not anticipated was that there was going to be such a huge queue outside the station. Everyone was trying to get out. I don't think anyone had thought about that.

Although the dates and times of this mad journey are long lost, what we do know is that on 10th June 1940 the Prime Minister Paul Reynaud and de Gaulle left Paris, his ministers fled the next day and a horde of Parisians in their millions followed suit. Lynn Olson, who wrote *Last Hope Island*, called it 'an anthill that had been knocked over'. The Germans arrived, unopposed, on 14th June, and Hitler came to crow over his latest conquest ten days later so we must have been a few days ahead of them, but not by very many.

This is the point when I remember Charles disappearing from my memory. I think he must have gone back to Britain via some other route because I don't remember him after that: with his SOE connections I suspect he was squirreled out of there on a plane before it was too late.

The swastika seen flying over Paris, June 1940. We must have missed the occupation by days.

As we queued to get into St-Lazare, there was a terrible air raid over Paris, non-stop banging, bombs dropping, exploding; the whole of Paris was in complete chaos.' My mother said, 'Oh, it's just fireworks, darling', but I knew it was all bombs, terrible bombs dropping all the time. And still everyone was saying to my mother, 'What are you doing here with a child?' We just managed to get onto the train. We must have hit the right queue by chance.

We were back on another train being attacked: terrible raids, constant bombing, the whole way to the coast. I don't go on a train very much these days, but if I do, I have a flashback to those journeys across Europe: the cattle truck full of people, these fingers coming out, the officials lashing out with their whips, hitting people onto or off the train, the bombings. It makes the 7.47 from Newbury to Waterloo look positively civilised.

At Le Havre we kept struggling forward. The men were very kind to us, because not only were there no children, there were hardly any women. They all gave way to my mother and me; we were helped on the boat, not thrown off. It was a British boat. We fought our way to the Union Jack. This time my mother made sure *everyone* could hear her talking in English... There were hordes of British soldiers who had been abandoned, trying to get on board. We scrambled past with their help.

The boat was jampacked, hundreds of people crammed together, standing room only. My mother was sitting on the floor, exhausted, propped up by a couple of soldiers. They were quite handsome and she certainly had an eye for a good-looking man – that kept her going. They were all clustered around her.

The crossing was very rough, lots of people were being sick: a *leitmotiv* of my whole journey from London to Stockholm and Russia and beyond.

And then, we saw England. The excitement, the screaming, the yelling. But the journey was still not over. We disembarked and the trains had stopped running. It was late. So we spent a night on the streets waiting for the morning trains. Yet again, everything was queues, queues. And no organisation. Finally we found ourselves on a train to Waterloo. We were met and taken to New Cavendish Street. This leg of the journey was over.

The person who was absolutely frantic by this time was my Swedish father, because to all intents and purpose we had completely disappeared;

he went mad, yelled and carried on. That would have been normal. To be honest I was quite glad to have escaped that...

I was now back in London, at the Hambros' house in New Cavendish Street. The city was not yet being blighted by the Blitz. The Battle of Britain was still some weeks away, but the Dunkirk evacuation was in full swing. Nonetheless, however quiet things were on the surface, the threat of invasion was omnipresent. Given the collapse of the British Expeditionary Force in France, not only was invasion possible, it seemed highly probable. The mood was exactly like it had been in Stockholm.

Events at Dunkirk triggered another round of evacuations for children living in London and the other major British cities. My mother and Charles – who had also made it back safely from Paris – and the other adults in the Mackay and Hambro families began another round of concocting plans, this time to remove the youngest children, including me, well out of potential harm's way.

My mother was also dealing with a huge personal trauma within the Mackay family: her beloved brother Ferrier had killed himself in February 1940. He had been depressed for a long time. Mama's father Alexander had died in 1936, at the age of 80, and in the absence of his calming, stabilising influence, Ferrier started unravelling. He had been living at Glencruitten, but then travelled over to Florida. The letters he sent back home from there were increasingly desperate, scribbled in pencil, barely readable. A chicken farm he was running had crashed; he was swindled out of a lot of money, and was effectively bankrupt. He was drinking heavily, smoking 60 cigarettes a day, a mess.

He and his wife Grace returned in May 1939, back to Glencruitten. He was now too old – and clearly not well enough – to be called up. In any case he had served in the Essex Regiment during the First World War, although his regiment never went to the frontline in France. Rupert Brooke was a friend of his. Although there was no shell shock to blame, Ferrier had obviously had existing mental issues. In 1928 he had been to hospital for treatment for a year. My grandfather received quantities of letters saying, 'I hope your son is feeling better'; he must have had some kind of nervous breakdown. When he committed suicide – he died from a self-inflicted gunshot wound – it was covered up. The official line passed down to the rest of the family was that Ferrier had died 'on manoeuvres'. My mother never ever talked to me about what happened. The war took people's lives in many different ways.

As it is difficult to find specific dates for this period of my life – records were destroyed, moves were frequent, diaries disappeared – I can at least identify one particular day, thanks to Frances Partridge's diary skills. She and my mother had kept in touch after Cambridge. In the King's College, Cambridge archive of the Bloomsbury Group are Frances Partridge's photo albums and diaries.

One photo shows her and my mother on their final day at Newnham, dressed up and ecstatic. There is also Frances's tiny leather-bound Walkers Graphic Diary for 1922, after they had both graduated, which shows that Doie had supper and tea with her or stayed over every few weeks that year, and in September they had a walking holiday in the Dolomites with Frances's sister Eleanor.

They had also been up to Oban together in August the year before: there is a photo of them up at the ruins of Gleyn Castle, a one-time stronghold of the MacDougalls, on the Isle of Kerrara, the island just offshore, which J. M. W. Turner had made multiple sketches of 90 years earlier.

In Frances's wartime diaries, she started 1940 with a timely observation (she called it a *bon mot*) from her husband Ralph Partridge, who was lying in bed: 'Time and weather are the hoary old beaters who put up us pheasants for the guns of God.' In April she heard the news about Britain's complete withdrawal of troops from Norway: 'The effect on me was crushing and bewildering. I felt even physically sick. Another country to be "mopped up" by the Germans.' Despite this, the day after, she noted that 'In contrast to all this it has been the most lovely and sweet May day, blue and green of the purest.'

A few weeks later, on Sunday 23rd June an old friend, recently returned from war-torn Europe, arrived. 'A hurly-burly of people began to arrive about 3.30. First Hambros (Dot, and Charles, Pam and Ann Mari) all turned up in a car from Marlborough, and poured into the sitting-room. Dot looked worn and thin, and said she still had a bumping heart and was terrified of raids.' My mother revealed her plans for us to be sent to North America: 'She was thinking of going to Canada with the children. Charles said by way of a candid concession that he "didn't mind saying he wished they all, he included, were steaming up the River St. Lawrence at this moment."' Ralph Partridge observed, 'which is true', that one couldn't help liking Charles.

A few days later again, Frances Partridge wrote, 'The general *dégringolade* of sense and wits, into stupidity, crass suspicion and suggestibility, the lunatic sheepishness bred by this war are almost as bad as the brutality and destruction.'

Ralph and Frances Partridge, Ham Spray, June 1940, symbolically feeding their white doves (they were ardent pacifists) while having the 'warmongering Hambros' to stay.

CHAPTER NINE

◆

NEW YORK CITY

The Morgan family Brownstone Mansion, at 231 Madison Avenue, New York.

I DID NOT HAVE long to enjoy being 'home', perhaps a couple of months at the most, before we were on our way again, travelling across the Atlantic.

As well as wishing us out of the way of bomb raids on London, there may also have been another reason. Jane Dismore, in her biography of Pamela Hambro, suggested that Charles might have been concerned about his family's Jewish ancestry.

There were five of us in the party: my mother, my stepsister Pammie, stepbrother Charlie and little Sally, only 18 months old. Mama was leaving her husband, engaged in top-secret war work, just as she had had to leave Marc and Peter in Sweden. She might well never have seen any of them again. I don't know quite how she coped with this continuous string of wrenching, distressing departures.

Unlike the glamorous pre-War voyages on the *Mauretania* or the *Olympic*, this time there were going to be no trunks full of evening gowns or dinner jackets. Rather than being serenaded by crooners and string orchestras, we were accompanied by enemy U-boats. There were two hits on our particular convoy, two ships torpedoed from under our noses.

Our ship was the *Empress Of Bermuda*. She was hugely overcrowded; you could hardly move on the boat. I later learnt it was carrying four times

SS *Empress of Bermuda*, part of the Canadia Shipping Steamship Company, sailing out of Southampton on its way to Halifax, Nova Scotia.

the normal number of passengers, including some German POWs. And what I did not know at the time was the *City Of Benares*, the equivalent evacuee passenger ship in one of the previous convoys (if not the one immediately before ours) had been sunk by a U-Boat torpedo, killing 73 of the 90 children on board.

The five of us bundled ourselves into one cabin with four bunks. Charlie and I had to budge up and sleep in the same bunk. Sally was teething, and fractious most of the time. Because there were so many passengers, there had to be three sittings for every meal. If you were in the third sitting, the food had pretty well run out, so we took it in turns. Also on board were a large number of unaccompanied children, who ran riot. All the children had a great time! The few grown-ups could not control us. For the kids it was an adventure, for me yet another adventure.

Pammie said that this crossing was the first time she had a taste of alcohol. There was a young man on board who took a shine to her and invited her to join him at one of the bars. She was happy to, but didn't know what to choose when he asked her what she'd like to drink. She made a decision based entirely on colour: 'Mm, I'll have that green one,' she said, pointing to one of the bottles on display. It turned out to be *crème de menthe*. She downed a few glasses, whereupon she was obliged to make her excuses and teeter back to her cabin, feeling somewhat the worse for wear... Cue one extremely disappointed admirer.

The ship eventually docked in Halifax, Nova Scotia. This may or not have been our intended destination – Mama's grandfather had after all been a prominent clergyman in Nova Scotia. He had been part of a significant Scottish diaspora to that particular province: in the early 1870s Scottish Presbyterians represented nearly 16% of the entire Canadian population, and over a quarter of Nova Scotia's.

The Rev. Robert Ferrier Burns (not *that* Robert Burns!) had come to Canada at the age of 18 when his father – my great-great-grandfather – also Robert Burns, an avid supporter of missionary support to the Scottish migrants who were seeking a new life in the New World, migrated himself, to Toronto. Ferrier was the maiden name of Robert Burns senior's wife. A nice footnote: she was the aunt of Susan Edmonstone Ferrier, a successful novelist, recently rediscovered by the likes of the crime writer Val McDermid, as 'Scotland's Jane Austen'.

Robert Ferrier Burns, after studying at Knox College in Toronto, was a minister in Montreal and Chicago before being inducted as the pastor of Fort Massey Church, Halifax, in 1875 – built as its name suggests on the site of an old military redoubt on top of Windmill Hill. He was later described by C. Prescott McLennan, one of his flock, as 'a Happy-Minded Scotsman... an extremely bulky man in bodily girth if not in height'. Apparently the climb up to the church was quite steep and hard work, especially in the winter when snow and ice coated the hill. On one occasion, Rev. Burns had been dragged up on a sledge but the rope snapped and he hurtled back downhill, quite cheerfully, demonstrating that 'unaffected and overflowing cheerfulness of a naturally radiant disposition', which led to him being described as a 'Professor of Optimism'.

After he retired in 1892, the Reverend came back to Scotland, settling in Brought Ferry (where my grandparents were living). In a family publication, *The Seaview Gazette*, he wrote that he was now 'comfortably settled in our lovely summer quarters by the sea – close to where the expanding Firth of Tay merges in the German ocean'. He was happy to be back in Scotland, but missed Halifax, saying it was 'hard to repress our deep regret as the beautiful city of the sea faded from our view.'

It was while Rev. Burns and his family were in Halifax that my grandmother Edith (the third of his eight children) learnt to play the organ. The use of any kind of external instrument had for centuries been anathema to the strict laws of the Presbyterians, but in 1873 the church had acquired a melodeon for the Sunday School, and in ten years later a pipe organ was installed behind the pulpit.

The first organist was my grandmother. She met my Mackay grandfather in Leipzig when she was on a trip to Germany, where she had gone to study music. Alexander's sister was staying in the same city. Apparently Edith and Alexander's sister were living in guest houses on the opposite sides of a street, and they rigged up some kind of telephone system so they could chat and share confidences. As a result Alexander knew how much music mattered to Edith, and he had the organ at Glencruitten built so she could carry on playing.

Our stay in Halifax was brief, but where we were heading from Nova Scotia was unclear. I found a letter from my mother, written from Halifax to her mother, saying, 'I don't really know what is going to happen to us. We have got nowhere to go.'

Eventually we found ourselves on a train heading south into the United States. Off the train's lengthy corridors were compartments, rather like old-fashioned drawing rooms, containing bunks covered by curtains. Quite often we got muddled and went into the wrong one by mistake, disturbing some puzzled stranger. It was summertime, and the heat was intense, so it was an uncomfortable journey.

The train terminated at Grand Central Station in New York. We disembarked and there outside the station, waiting for us, were three gorgeous Cadillacs, each with gleaming white-wall tyres, and a suited chauffeur, sent to collect us by the J.P Morgan family. The Morgans and the Hambros were long-time friends. Jack Morgan, then head of J.P Morgan, had lived in England for eight years at the turn of the century and became great friends with Eric Hambro – my stepfather's father.

Grand Central Station, New York, in 1940.

Together they bought Gannochy, the 17,000-acre estate near Edzell in Angus, where Charles had courted his first wife, Pamela.

According to my future brother-in-law Andrew Gibson-Watt, 'the Hambros had always maintained a strong friendship with the American banking family of Morgan. When the going got tough in 1940, Harry

Morgan sent a cable to Charles Hambro, saying in effect, "Send as many as you like…" Charles was already occupying a well-informed position, and he thought his country's survival at best problematical.'

My stepfather had arranged everything with Harry and Catherine Morgan. Harry was Jack Morgan's son, had been born in London, and after graduating from Harvard, started working in the family bank, initially as a $15-a-day messenger boy, before co-founding Morgan Stanley in the late 1930s. He was described by a biography of the Morgan family as 'all thrusting energy, his chin assertive, his lips tightly compressed, his gaze fiery.' His wife was Catherine Adams, a direct descendant of two US Presidents, John Adams and John Quincy Adams.

My mother had known that there was a chance the Morgans would help us, but she was worried because when we arrived in Halifax, she still had not heard a word from them: in the letter she had written to my grandmother from Nova Scotia, she said had a back-up plan to contact a friend of hers, Dorothy Breck, who she was sure would take us in if all else failed. Not knowing whether everything had been settled, my mother must have been in a state of nerves.

It was extraordinary to arrive in New York, this war-free, frenetic metropolis that I had only ever seen in movies, to find this fantastically elegant couple, dressed to the nines, and their three limousines with chauffeurs. We really looked like refugees. Charlie had holes in his socks – Mama had never threaded a needle or darned anything in her life – and my mother was the worst: normally such an elegant woman, her hair was all over the place.

It was the second year of the New York World's Fair in Flushing Meadows. As we drove out to Long Island where the Morgans had a house, we passed the Fair, illuminated by what seemed a million lights. There were fireworks going off. Exhausted, and disorientated, I found it all completely bamboozling.

We were taken to 'Maple Knoll', a relatively new manor house near Syosset, with an 8-car garage for all those Cadillacs. They had five sons, the youngest about the same age as Sally, the oldest around 16 or so.

Above: Henry Sturgis and Catherine Morgan in the late Eighties.

Opposite top: Maple Knoll House, the Morgan family home
in Locust Valley, Long Island, NY.

Opposite below: Blended family 1941: Back row from left to right:
John Adams Morgan, Ann Mari Wallenberg, Charlie Hambro, Miles Morgan,
Catherine Morgan, Henry Morgan, Charles Francis Morgan, Pamela Hambro,
Harry Morgan Jr. Front row: Peter Angus Morgan, Sally Hambro.

LOCUST VALLEY
LONG ISLAND, NEW YORK

The boys were paraded before us, looking extremely displeased: they didn't want us in the slightest, which made for a tricky atmosphere.

John Adams Morgan, the fourth of the five sons, who was a year or so younger than me, and about the same age as Charlie, although remembering that we arrived, does not remember any significant impact on his world. I think we were an insignificant blip in their way of life – whereas the effect on us was huge – and in addition they were used to a round of house guests they didn't know turning up at the house. They simply got on with being Morgans.

We were not the only wartime guests of the extended family. Harry's father Jack had welcomed into his mansion at Matinecock Point, a couple of miles away, the young Lord Primrose, son of the Earl of Rosebery, and two grandsons of Lord Bicester.

In the Morgan family biography, my stepbrother Charlie is quoted as saying, 'Jack Morgan lived in considerable Victorian splendour, with armed guards all over the place'. The Morgans certainly valued their privacy, and were also very sensitive about the possibility of kidnappings, especially after the taking and murder of Charles Lindbergh's son, an incident the Morgan family had been only too aware of, both as friends of Lindbergh, and as the bankers who prepared and numbered the ransom money.

Other expat refugees included Rose and Jemima Pitman, who stayed with Junius Morgan at his estate called Salutation in Glen Cove, where from time to time they were visited by Ian Fleming, in his pre-Bond guise as a Naval Intelligence Department officer liaising with his American counterparts (Junius was in the OSS, the Office of Strategic Services, a forerunner of the CIA). Fleming knew the Pitmans as he had worked for the stockbroking company Rowe & Pitman before the war: his own assessment was as 'the world's worst stockbroker'. And the Pitmans were friends of Junius: they were all mad about shooting.

Almost as soon as we arrived Harry and Catherine Morgan breezily said, 'Goodbye, we're off on vacation' – to Arizona or somewhere – and left us, a gaggle of dirty, smutty, raggle-taggle Brits, in the capable, unflappable hands of their butlers along with a very fierce governess, who had been a matron at one of those very tough Scottish boarding schools.

The Morgan family also owned a brownstone house in New York, bang opposite the marble splendour of the Morgan Library on Madison Avenue and a couple of blocks from the Empire State Building. We were moved in there, so that we could go to school once term started.

The Morgan Library's collection had been created by Harry Morgan's grandfather Pierpoint, a passionate collector, who had amassed the largest private art collection of the day. The Library contained heaps of fantastic things: furniture, artworks, prints, rare manuscripts. But oddly it turned out the rest of the Morgan family, compared to Pierpoint, were total philistines – they were not interested in the Library at all, so my mother took us there instead.

It feels terrible to say that, because they were so incredibly kind to take us in, but we would solemnly sit at dinner every night, with no interesting conversation at all. It was stultifying. I think Mama died of boredom. Every day was the same, very unsociable, virtually no visitors, hardly one dinner party. She said it was the most excruciating time of her life. She either kept her brain stimulated by going to art galleries and museums, or numbed the tedium with plenty of alcohol – everyone started drinking pretty early in the day.

One day, however, there had been a visitor to the brownstone, shortly after we arrived. I was going down the stairs and glancing through the open door of the dining room saw that the table had been laid for a lunch party. I went upstairs, and asked one of the Morgans' multiple minions what was happening. It turned out to be a lunch in honour of my Swedish father, who was in town on business. He was in the States on behalf of the Swedish government, armed with a handy diplomatic passport and tasked with explaining to the Americans in Washington how tricky Sweden's situation was. And of course he and Charles Hambro were in constant contact about us because they had a joint interest with their children.

Like my mother's magical appearance at the front door of the Stockholm flat, I did not understand the reason why my father was suddenly in New

On the doorstep at Maple Knoll, left to right: Ann Mari, Charlie, Doie, Sally and Pammie.

The luxury of a swimming pool and hot weather! John Morgan jumping in, Sally Hambro and Angus Morgan in the foreground.

York. Once again I though this this really was too much serendipity. But that was my life, though: these extraordinary happenings, I call them.

Pammie and I were sent to an enormous, wonderful, girls' school, the Brearley, on the Upper East Side right next to the East River. Our playground was a huge concrete edifice that hung over the river; the tugboats would stop and toot at us and the boatmen shouted inaudible, doubtless ribald, comments. It took us a little while to acclimatise, but then we simply adored it there. One classmate of Pammie's, Franny Parsons, remembered hearing Pammie recite Matthew Arnold's 'Dover Beach' and being deeply moved 'by her beautiful English voice'.

The Morgans found us an apartment two minutes' walk away, where we were controlled by Miss Macdonald, the very fierce ex-boys' school matron, who had been in charge of the Morgan boys. Another nanny looked after Sally, my baby sister, and Angus, the youngest of the Morgan boys, and they were usually off in Washington, where Harry Morgan was involved with the Navy, so we had this whole apartment to ourselves, in one of the smartest possible areas. And we took it all for granted, I think.

In that first term at Brearley, the USA was in the throes of a presidential election. Franklin D. Roosevelt was aiming for his third term, up against the Republican nominee Wendell Wilkie. Everyone at school was sporting huge buttons, and we were virtually the only ones out of the entire 700 pupils who wore a Roosevelt button, because my mother said, 'Roosevelt will bring America into the war'. To top it all the Morgans were backing Wilkie.

Every morning at school we were meant to stand and salute the Stars and Stripes and sing 'God Bless America', but Mama told us we were not to do that obeisance to America until they came into the war. She said we had to stay sitting down, which we did. Eventually Pammie and I were carted off to the headmistress who said she would, exceptionally, give us special permission to be let off. She only told a few teachers; however, one or two of them did later come up to me: 'I hear you don't salute the flag'. This was typical of my mother, she was always very political, a throwback to her growing up in Glencruitten, the sisters arguing and slamming doors, egged on by Alexander.

I had an ongoing banter with the elevator boy in our apartment block: he was quite good-looking, and became a friend. We Brits all thought the Americans would rush to come into the war, especially after the Japanese attack on Pearl Harbor. But the liftboy was an isolationist through and through, typical of so many Americans at the time. I would tease him, saying, 'But you keep saying the Brits are your best friends, why don't you want to help us?' He would say right back, 'Oh, we don't want to get involved in all that crap.'

Brearley had a reputation as a liberal arts school – old girls include Jill Clayburgh, Caroline Kennedy and Niki de Saint-Phalle, as well as Oona O'Neill, the daughter of Eugene, who joined Brearley in 1940 and married Charlie Chaplin a month after she turned 18. Consequently all the pupils had to take part in the school plays, and learn an instrument to perform in the orchestra however good or bad you were, a wonderful ethic. There was no question of saying no to that. We all played the piano and I also took up the viola, which meant about one squeaky stroke and that was it. I was hopeless... By the time I was 18 I had been to seven schools. Brearley was the only one I stayed at for any length of time. I made some really good friends there whom I still keep in touch with.

After six months, my mother went back to London. She managed to get a berth on a ship going to Lisbon. In Portugal, there was another bureaucratic mix-up, and she was stuck there without any money, and no obvious way of getting to England. She was sitting in desperation, when my father Marcus walked in to the hotel lobby. It was total chance. He was there on some government mission. My mother rushed up to him, threw her arms round his neck and said, 'Can you pay our bill?' He bailed her out, she stayed another two days and then went back by plane; he paid for their flights as well. It's a good job they were still on speaking terms.

I understood why she left. She wanted to get back to Charles: they had really not spent much of their married life together, and she knew we were in safe hands. I don't think my younger sister, Sally, ever really forgave her for leaving us, although it made no difference to our daily life. We were being so well looked after. Every day we were asked what we would like to eat, and this was prepared a properly trained cook, an Irishwoman if I remember rightly. I kept telling Sally this is what these people gave us and did for us, but she felt that Mama should have been there for us. We have always argued about it.

The day after Mama left New York, Mrs Morgan lined us all up and said, 'I don't want any goddamn bad behaviour'. She swore like a trooper: we had never heard anything like it. Although she was a tough cookie, she was extraordinarily generous to us: we had no money.

As a direct descendant of the Adams: she was what we called 'American grand', from that group of old New England families called the Boston Brahmins, who seemed to come from a much earlier age, When we went to visit her mother, who lived in Boston, the maids had long dresses down to the ground. It all felt very old-fashioned to us. The Adams spoke a certain sort of American, with a Bostonian twang, which was very distinctive, and very different from the New York American accent. I remember in particular the way she pronounced the word 'laundry' – it was more like 'landry'.

We carried on with our New York life in our apartment and at the Brearley school. At the weekends the Morgans would be at their house on Long Island, and although we would join them there occasionally we spent most of our time in Manhattan, as they preferred not to have any children around. Their weekends were all about shooting the pheasants raised on their estate: blood sports were a large part of that social scene.

So we were enrolled in something called the Saturday Club, for children who were left alone in the city. The club kept us busy. We played a lot of tennis, and lacrosse, which I hated – a dreadful game... Afterwards the great thing was to go to Hamburger Heaven, where they did have the best hamburgers in the whole of New York, if not the entire world. This was indeed the life.

◇

CHAPTER TEN

◈

LONG JOURNEY HOME

Paradise Flat, the Pennoyer family estate in Lake Tahoe, CA.

IN 1943, three years after arriving in New York, it was time to return. The real reason we had to was that Pammie had developed anorexia. We did not really know what it was she was suffering with, but she suddenly plummeted down to six stone. She was 5 foot 10, and she looked dreadful.

This had all come about because she was caught up in a love triangle. On our arrival in the States, Harry Morgan Jr, the eldest of the Morgan boys had taken a fancy to Pammie. Alas for Harry his love was not reciprocated. Nonetheless he persevered. He had just got his own car, and so I always had to go in the car with them as the spare wheel, which drove me mad. Of course, at one level, we were completely seduced by the sheer Americanism of it all, teenage boys with smart cars. But Pammie simply did not fancy him.

Then things got complicated because she fell for Harry's cousin Bob Pennoyer, and this made Harry Jr absolutely furious, since he considered Pammie to be his personal property. Tensions didn't just simmer, they boiled over.

Bob Pennoyer was also a grandson of J.P Morgan Jr. (born in his house on the corner of 37th Street). The Pennoyers were Huguenots, by way of Normandy and Wales and eventually California. Bob's father Paul went to Harvard, and thence Harvard Law School, and via her brother Julius met Frances, J.P.'s youngest daughter. He took her back to California and Frances was enchanted.

Bob grew up in a world of wealth, privilege and security. He and his sister were driven in chauffeured cars along long driveways for playdates. 'My grandfather lived in a cocoon like a feudal lord.'

Unlike my own Mackay grandfather, J.P., three decades on, did not believe in education for women. 'College was out of the question.. He considered that it unsexed a woman.' Bob remembers the same Sunday dinners, five courses, rigidly programmed, black tie and evening dress, a footman behind each chair. 'They were neither convivial nor congenial, especially being paraded along the long hall to the dining room.'

Bob later wrote about the moment he met Pammie. 'My sister Jessie brought a friend from Brearley School: Pamela Hambro, a classically beautiful girl.' This might have been for a Christmas night dinner on Long Island since we were often staying with Harry Morgan on Long Island, not far from where Bob's family (who had a swimming pool) were based; through the following spring there were many subsequent gatherings, swimming parties. Within a short space of time 'I had fallen headlong in love with Pammie, and she with me.' Bob remembers their first kiss, when Pammie was 16: he was driving her in an old Ford either to or back from the Harry Morgan house when they pulled up in a convenient, secluded lane.

She visited Bob at Harvard a couple of times: his room-mate gave a party for them. In 1941, and again in 1942, he took Pammie to the Pennoyers' place at Paradise Flat, north of Emerald Bay on the west shore of Lake Tahoe in California, a three-day train journey. There was no hanky panky allowed: Bob's mother ripped back the curtain of the sleeping compartment at one inconvenient moment. At Paradise Flat there were hikes and camp-outs in the Sierras, fishing and tennis, and some skinny-dipping when parents were otherwise engaged. Bob and Pammie were about to turn 18, and were talking about wanting to get married.

But the Harry Morgan Jr issue was still there. Bob recalls that Harry Jr

Lunch alfresco in Paradise Flat.

was 'a brute, with a passion for knives and guns. His college room-mates were terrified of him.' There was a certain amount of social scorn involved too: from Bob's point of view the Morgans looked down on the Pennoyers. And although Harry Jr and his parents were usually at loggerheads, in this instance, they took their son's side, which led to endless tension.

My sister was in the middle of this, and I was bored to death because I heard nothing else: 'And do you know what he said now?'...

Pammie's health continued to get worse. She looked awful, so miserable, incredibly skinny, her bones sticking out, everything we now automatically associate with anorexia, but which at the time was not properly understood. There was no name for it. The doctor thought she was dying – I think he was absolutely right in his assessment – and the Morgans said they could not take responsibility for us any more.

The first that Bob Pennoyer heard about this was in early 1943. He had just lost his grandfather; his older brother had got married. He was feeling a little raw in any case. 'I had come home one weekend, in midshipman's uniform, and was out walking with my mother when she broke the news that Pammie would be returning to England in March. There were tears streaming down her face. It was the only time I ever saw my mother cry.' A week before she left, Bob and Pammie went to watch Casablanca at the movies. 'I left her at Penn Station, where she took the train to Philadelphia' and from there headed for a boat to Lisbon. 'My ardent hopes went with her.'

Bob was heart-broken and sent a raft of letters to London. Eventually he received a letter from Charles Hambro, asking him 'to stop sending letters, or I'll let your parents know.' Pammie and Bob did see each other again, but only fifty years later, in which time Bob had served with distinction in the US Navy in the Pacific, watching the Marines raise the flag at Iwo Jima, before becoming a succesful lawyer.

Bob Pennoyer.

Bob and Pammie married other people (Pammie married twice) but they kept in touch and met up in the early 2000s. Luckily Bob's wife Vicky got on famously with Pammie, and Pammie's second husband Andrew and Bob also clicked.

Some sixty years after this all happened, it was clear that their relationship had been important to both of them. In 2004 Pammie wrote to Bob, 'I am so thankful that you feel the same about our lovely youthful friendship. I was afraid that you might hate me for my unforgiveable behaviour! I really did adore you, you know. I think my return to a war-torn country and my family who I had not seen for nearly three years was the reason that my love for you, though not forgotten, had to fade, in the light of a new life and new friends and a feeling of slight desperation that one was not going to ever have life the same again.'

Bob replied, 'I shall always love you for the happiness we shared when we were very young. I was astonished to hear you say that you thought I might have hated you for your unforgivable behaviour... because I never felt anything but the deepest affection for you. The war that brought us

Crowding onto the Serpa Pinto, bound for Lisbon.

together was bound to take us apart. I was too young to fulfil the promise of a life together. Losing you was one of the hardest things I ever had to face.'

For me this time out of time in New York, three years in the lap of luxury, in the heart of Manhattan, the most stable and happiest of my life to date, were over.

It was arranged that Charlie and I were going to be travelling to Britain together, Pamela having returned separately some weeks earlier with Sally, who was now five years old. There was some sensible planning behind splitting us up. My father and stepfather did not want us all to be on the same boat because of the fear of torpedoing, which was still a threat to all those boats crossing the Atlantic.

While Pammie and I had had such a wonderful time at Brearley, Charlie had been bunged off to the Groton School in Massachusetts. Groton was an Episcopal boarding school for boys that prided itself on a Spartan brand of 'muscular Christianity' involving a regime of cold showers, and counted Franklin D. Roosevelt, Dean Acheson, William

Averell Harriman among its old boys, as well as Harry Morgan, hence Charlie's attendance. As he had been sent off to Groton almost as soon as we arrived, and in the holidays he was off with the Morgan boys, I had hardly seen anything of him, which was awful, since we had been so close.

We were heading back to a Europe in the midst of a war that in 1943 still showed no clear sign of reaching a conclusion, although now we left the United States behind as a powerful ally rather than the country we had arrived in when it was hovering in an ambivalent neutrality. I waved goodbye to the Morgans, the brownstone, Brearley School, and the Cadillacs and their chauffeurs.

We were placed on a ship heading for Portugal, the *Serpa Pinto* – extraordinary that I can instantly remember that name over seventy years later. The *Serpa Pinto* was a former British steamship which had been converted into a liner for a Portuguese shipping line, and since 1940 had been plying back and forth between Lisbon and Brazil, or Lisbon and New York. It became quite famous, since not only did it make more Atlantic crossings than any other civilian vessel during the War, but on the leg from Europe to the Americas transported some 110,000 refugees, especially Jewish families fleeing from the Nazis. Marcel Duchamp, Simone Weil and the future Rebbe, Menachem Mendel Schneerson, all travelled to the US on the *Serpa Pinto*, which became known as the *navio de amizade*, the ship of friendship.

Our crossing was uneventful. We sailed through the Atlantic without any trouble, and had a wonderful time onboard. One of the next ships to make the crossing was sunk with all the children on board, so we were jolly lucky there.

However, exactly like the journey with Mama and Charles across Europe in 1940, this trip ended up being fraught with additional digressions and delays. When we reached Lisbon, there was a problem. It transpired that my age had been incorrectly entered on some document or other as 41, not 14 – so they decided I was an adult who was accompanying Charlie. The situation was exacerbated because my surname was Wallenberg, and the authorities therefore assumed that I was Charlie Hambro's

Swedish nanny or governess rather than his stepsister. At that point only unaccompanied children were being allowed back to England. We found ourselves stuck there for three weeks.

Charlie and I were completely alone, in a reasonably smart hotel in a seafront suburb of Lisbon, where all the *Serpa Pinto* children had been billeted for two or three days on arrival before they moved on to England. All the other children departed, and then we were the only two left there, alone, with no grown-ups to help, and virtually no money. Every morning we walked down to the lobby to ask what was happening: we were told to get in touch with this or that person who would let us know when we were going, but the answer was always vague and non-committal. Day after day we asked, 'Any news?' and there was none. We were in danger of being completely forgotten.

Then we ran out of money to pay the hotel bill. Although the Morgans had been as ever very generous and given us money for our expenses on the trip, they naturally thought we were only going to need enough to tide us over for a few days.

We had to find some other accommodation and we could only afford somewhere cheap. We walked up and down the nearby streets, banging on any doors which seemed to offer bed and breakfast. Most of them turned us down: they wanted adult guests, not children. Eventually some kind lady, in a long pitch-black dress, listened to my pleading. She had one room with a small bed in it. We snapped up her offer.

The days we spent there are rather a blur. Charlie, who was 13, started behaving very badly, smoking like a chimney. With some of our dwindling stash of money we went to the cinema: in a nearby park afterwards he recklessly used a peashooter he had acquired to flip the hats off the heads of some German soldiers. He was only having fun, trying to keep himself amused, but it was a dangerous game to play. Like Stockholm, and New York in 1940, Lisbon was another great neutral city, one of the last free ports on the Continent, but it was populated with pro-Allies and pro-Axis spies and agents. Later I discovered Charlie had gone by himself to the local casino. I don't know how he managed to get in; I was really worried about him.

The Boeing 314 clipper that met us at Southampton.

One day the great news finally came through that we were being allowed to leave. We flew in a seaplane, and arrived on the Solent at Southampton. Incidentally that seaplane was shot down the next time it made the trip, the last in a line of near misses.

The final annoyance was that having made it to England, the British authorities would not let me in. We were held back and told to go to some sort of office when we arrived and I was then interrogated. I was on my own: they wouldn't even let Charlie into the room. I had a lamp shone into my face, a real movie-type interrogation. It lasted for hours. I was only 14. It was all about me being Swedish, and why was I there, and why was I with this English boy? They went on and on, and I kept giving the same answer each time, and saying, 'Why don't you ring up my stepfather Charles Hambro?' Charlie for his part tried telling the officials, 'But she is my half-sister...' They didn't listen. Somebody must eventually have believed us because we were put on a train to London. We just couldn't believe it when we arrived at Waterloo and there were my mother and stepfather, Pamela and little Sally, all waiting on the platform. They were absolutely beside themselves with worry because they had met every single train after the seaplane had landed not knowing that we were held up. It was a fantastic moment, a wonderful reunion.

◇

CHAPTER ELEVEN

WARTIME LONDON AND ELSEWHERE

Dixton Manor, Gloucestershire, in 1946.

THE RETURN TO wartime London provided a distinct shock to my system, emotional, mental and physical. For three years in the gilded avenues of New York I had been thoroughly pampered, eating wonderful food. Overnight I was being fed what could be scraped together from the ration books. We found the food quite disgusting; it made us ill.

My mother also received a shock: we came back complete with broad American accents. And straightaway we were complaining like anything about the way things were in England. Mama just said endlessly, 'Jolly good for you, you've been spoilt to death for three years.' And she was right; it was extremely good for us.

Only Pammie had truly suffered, with her crushed romance, and her eating disorder. Andrew Gibson-Watt, who would later become her second husband, met her shortly after her return. 'She had an intriguing American accent and was obviously going to be an exceptionally beautiful girl: but for the time being she was suffering from an unwillingness to eat, and looked painfully thin and strained.' She had escaped a direct V1 hit on the Guards Chapel near St James's Park in June 1944 that killed 140: the Queen was – unusually – not in attendance, and for once Pammie was not there for the weekly Sunday service as she had a cold. She had managed to get through her anorexia – most of the hospitals in London had not wanted to take her, not really knowing how to cure her, but one hospital accepted her and tried out a new, tough regime on her, and that finally cured her, after three months or so.

England was so different; everything was different. The John Adam house on New Cavendish Street had been sold, and the Hambros' house in the country in Dorset, Hedge End – a remnant of the great estate that had been sold by Charles's father, Eric Hambro – had been taken over as a home for illegitimate children, many of them mixed race, the children of English girls and black GIs.

We moved into a cottage nearby which had no running water, just a well and a pump, and no heating. There was an extremely unattractive loo, a bucket of Elsan which we called the DLD, for Don't Look Down... Back in Sweden the Wallenbergs had something similar, a loo attached to a shooting lodge, which had no running water. You pulled a plug and a whole lot of sawdust would drop down. My grandmother was very economical, and would stand outside reminding me, 'One pull is quite enough'. We were constantly re-lighting lamps or boiling water for baths. Soap was virtually non-existent, so we used masses of soda to cut through the grease when we were washing up.

We couldn't complain; everyone was suffering. On the train down to Dorset from Paddington, we went past slums, standing back to back, and could see both adults and children with no shoes on, even in the depths of winter.

I longed to go back to school because having been dreaming about returning to the home we loved, it was all gone. I was sent to Queen's Gate School, which was normally based in South Kensington, but for the duration of the War had relocated to Downe House School, at Cold Ash near Newbury, while the Queen's Gate buildings were used for the London Auxiliary Fire Brigade.

The Queen's Gate principal, Miss Spalding – known as 'Spee' – was very outspoken, terribly worldly; she told us a series of racy stories (today they would seem very mild) which had us gripped. I can remember laughing in class – you didn't expect that when being prepared for confirmation. Miss Spalding was also actually interested in me, as a Swede and as a neutral.

It was not very nice coming back to England during the war and being called 'a bloody neutral', and often being maliciously teased about it. I felt the contrast quite keenly to the Hambros, this Establishment family who were important in their own sphere. I was an alien, and had to report to the police every three months, even as a 16 year-old. It was no fun, and one is particularly touchy as a teenager. It made me question my whole identity. Who the hell was I, in fact?

After my experiences over the previous few years, I initially found the other girls at school rather childish. I felt far more grown up. They were still pretending to be horses and jumping over things... What was amazing was that within six months I was jumping trees like horses with the best of them. I had regressed, or perhaps it was my survival system. After going to so many schools in different countries, I had become very good at adapting, I was always determined to make a go of it. I was on my own because Pammie, now 17, had got a secretarial job at the Ministry of Warfare.

The Downe House girls looked down terribly on the Queen's Gate intake. Another Queen's Gate pupil, Cherry Gibbs, was in the year above me. She thought the Downe House girls saw us either as London snobs or refugees, while we thought, rather unfairly, that they were country bumpkins.

There were only 60 of us and more than 300 of them, and we loathed each other. We were given the worst possible dorms you can imagine, no heating, no water, the loos always breaking down. I got boils and chilblains, and had to wear gloves indoors hardly able to grip a pen, it was so cold. Food was still an issue. We never saw one pat of butter the entire time we were at Downe House: we later found out that the teachers had taken all the butter rations for themselves.

The world of a British girl's boarding school was all a hell of a leap from being a day girl at an upmarket New York school. Of course my American accent made me a target. Cherry Gibbs distinctly remembers me turning up fresh from New York City, along with twin sisters called the Seymours, and what stood out most to the girls who had been stuck in England throughout the war, getting by on clothing rations, were our clothes, those loose jersey Sloppy Joes hanging down to our hips, and our shoes. For Cherry we brought across the Atlantic with us a glamorous, sassy flavour of Manhattan.

Those smart American clothes were, of course, thanks to the incredible generosity of the Morgans. My mother said that the Morgans had never asked for any financial contribution to the cost of looking after us all, which was extraordinary, especially given the fact we had been their guests for well over three years. I think that Catty Morgan – the mother of five boys – had been privately appalled by and rather nervous about the idea of looking after Pammie and me. She simply was not used to girls, and in fact she later told me that she was *absolutely* dreading the prospect when she heard we were arriving to stay. Eventually she did get used to having us there, and who knows may in the end have enjoyed going shopping with us, at Saks Fifth Avenue, naturally. She herself had hundreds of pairs of shoes which took up an entire room. Since we had the same size feet she would let me try them all on.

The great thing about being at Downe House was that we absolutely thrashed their girls at games, in everything from lacrosse to tennis, because Queen's Gate had some fantastically sporty girls. That was very good for morale. Oddly, when the Queen's Gate girls went back to London at the end of the war, we hated the place and our sense of cohesion was lost. At this time my parents had a flat in St John's Wood, in one of those Edwardian mansion blocks. Every day I would take the number 74 bus across town to school. By then we were all bobby soxers, smitten with Frank Sinatra; our Latin teacher sang with the Tommy Dorsey Orchestra and was in a chorus supporting Sinatra in London. We all got free tickets.

Meanwhile, Mama and Charles were trying to find another house. We bicycled for miles all over Gloucestershire; we children hated everything they looked at and said so. We must have been terribly tiresome. My poor mother. Having been longing for her children for nearly three years,

Doie and Charles Hambro, Dixton Manor, 1947.

she found that we were complete brats. Sally had been so young when Mama left New York that she did not really remember her mother. And my mother had still not seen either of my brothers since the day we left Stockholm, bravely going into the unknown.

While the search for a country house went on, for a while in this peripatetic lifestyle we spent time in Kent with old uncle Olaf at Linton Park near Maidstone. This house was a large, white mansion set high up on an escarpment looking out south across the Weald; Horace Walpole once wrote 'it stands like the citadel of Kent; the whole county is its garden.'

Olaf, a cousin of my stepfather's, had bought Linton Park in the late 1930s. He had a young man living with him for years – their relationship was, I think, platonic. However, one day, I found myself sitting next to this young man at dinner and asked him, 'Why aren't you married with a wife and children?' There was a dead silence round the table, not a word spoken for about ten minutes. After dinner I received a rocket from my mother.

The country house my mother and Charles finally settled on, and in, was Dixton Manor, near Alderton, a dozen miles or so north of Cheltenham. The house later passed on to my step-brother Charles and became something of a social magnet, a venue for smart house parties, courtesy of his wife, Cherry. She was a character, and had had a verse written for her by Noël Coward when she lived in the Caribbean: 'Now Little Cherry Huggins was a glamorous soubrette, And everyone adored her from the vicar to the vet. She seem to try with eagerness to pass her school exam, But everybody realised she didn't give a damn.'

Although it was a beautiful house, a Grade II listed manor built in 1555, I did not like Dixton, simply because I, like Charlie, had loved Hedge End, in comparison a rather ugly little Victorian farmhouse but with a marvellous garden. We were annoyed to find the house had been sold while we were away in the States. We adored Hedge End; consequently we abhorred Dixton, idyllic as it was. However, we came to appreciate it in the end. My nephew, Alexander Snow, owns it now and visits there remind me of the family atmosphere that my mother and stepfather worked so hard to create for us.

So weekends and holidays were now spent at Dixton, but despite our new settled state, change was in the air. There were the usual family traumas. Charles Hambro left his job as the head of SOE, and I was always concerned that it was for some awful reason, some unmentionable treachery. There was a nasty feeling in the air, which gave me a feeling that he had done something wrong. Only recently did I learn that it was in fact because of a policy disagreement and the goings-on by a rogue SOE cell, which gave the career military types the chance to manoeuvre out

Above: Dixton covered in snow; the winter of 1947 was the coldest on record.
Below: David Holman, Fay Donovan and Michael Bonsor at Dixton.
Opposite top: Sally Hambro on top of the gateposts at Dixton.
Opposite below: Doie, Fay Donovan, Michael Bonsor, David Holman and Charles Hambro having tea on the terrace at Dixton.

this banker they had never really taken to. It certainly affected Charles. He was not in good form, definitely unsettled. I picked up that things were not right, that he was not happy, perhaps from overhearing him talking to my mother.

The Mackay family had lost Ferrier, my uncle, in 1940, and my grandfather Alexander four years earlier. My grandmother Edith died after the War. She had stayed up in Glencruitten. We always loved her, even though she was so totally scatty. In her later life she had been crippled with arthritis (there were no painkillers then) and she rather let herself go. But she retained her terrific sense of humour throughout.

Among the Wallenbergs there had been different war experiences. I later learnt that my father and Uncle Jacob had worked with those in Germany who opposed the Nazis – Carl Goerdeler, the mayor of Leipzig, for example – to pass messages to the British government. The Ambassador to Sweden, Victor Mallet, recalled that my uncle Jacob, this brilliant banker and most patriotic Swede' had supplied valuable information, through his connections with Goerdeler and his comrades.

There was also a hiccup called the 'Bosch affair' that involved the British Ambassador Victor Mallet and my father, and which blew up at the end of the war. Jacob accepted responsibility, although he felt my father had been at fault.

Charles Hambro had been knighted: in his SOE days, he had overseen an undercover operation to extract vital ball bearings from Sweden, stuck in a Norwegian port. He had been the head of the British Raw Materials Mission, liaising with Washington, and in 1945 went into Germany with the ASOS mission to reach Germany's nuclear operations and laboratories. Sir Charles was now back at the helm of Hambros Bank.

One of Mama's best friends at Cambridge (they were contemporaries at Newnham) had been Frances Partridge of Bloomsbury Group fame. In those days, it was rather frowned on if you were homosexual, and given that many of the Bloomsbury set were very peculiar, let's say ambidextrous, my mother, despite not really approving, took it on board because she loved the idea of the Bloomsbury Group.

Charles sweeping the frozen pond for skating, winter at Dixton 1947.

My mother's sister, Elizabeth, the pianist, who I knew as Auntie Pooh, said that once they went round to dinner at one of the Bloomsbury Group's houses, extremely excited to meet these dazzling luminaries, and were disappointed to find their conversation was neither sparkling nor stimulating: 'They just spent all the time talking about their drains', she complained.

Frances Partridge was a pacifist, so she and Mama did not speak for much of the War. After VE Day, when this bone of contention was safely out of the way, they got back in regular contact. Frances was one of the great diarists, and in an entry in the 1960s she remembered having gone back to her old house in West Halkin Street and bumping into my mother, who was living in Cadogan Street. Her comment was that she thought Doie had changed, and had become 'a corporate wife'.

In May 1945 it was all over. As Frances Partridge wrote, 'We have sailed suddenly into a lagoon of peace and solitude.' By the time peace came, our world was completely altered, irrevocably changed.

But not everything changed. Throughout the rest of their lives Charles and Doie would dress for dinner, every night, whether guests were coming or they were dining alone. Black tie, a full-length gown, jewels, the works. At 7.15 a couple of stiff Martinis, wine with three courses, and for Charles a whisky afterwards. Some standards had to be maintained, even if outside the world was in a state of flux.

After taking my School Certificate at Queen's Gate, I was taken on something of a miniature Grand Tour by both my father and stepfather: to Milan, Florence, Ischia and Capri. These were recces by them to re-establish banking and business relationships in the wreckage of post-war Europe. I don't think Charles was still involved in espionage activities, but who knows? In one Italian city I saw my mother and stepsister Diana (who had come along with her husband David) chatting up a group of Italian men. 'How terrible, flirting openly like that', I thought, and stalked off in high-minded dudgeon. It turned out that the Italians were highly important and influential businessmen and Doie and Diana had been applying some charm to help Charles rustle up some deal or other.

The poverty in Italy was stark. The locals were often barefoot. There were hardly any tourists; hotels were just starting up again. The food (always a point of interest for me) was far better than in England, and the museums and galleries were extraordinary, with no queues or timeslots. You could just wander in. Although I sensed my parents were exhausted by the war and so did not feel as positive as I did, I decided to enjoy myself. I have memories of always sitting on top of taxis rather than in them... Yes, we were in the middle of the ravages of war, but I was seventeen, and to hell with social conscience. I had a damn good time.

Above: Doie and I trying out a gondola, Venice 1947.
Below: Diana and David Gibson-Watt and Doie, Siena 1947.

Charles and I sightseeing in Syracuse 1947.

In 1947 I went with my father to Latin America: Brazil, Chile and Argentina. Marianne Wallenberg and my step-sister Catharina came along on the trip, which was a testament to the cordial relationship between the two families. We flew with Scandinavian Airlines, not good old BOAC, in a series of short hops, up and over the North Pole where a party was thrown in the same way liners celebrate crossing the Equator. In Buenos Aires, Eva Perón was in full flow, on the balcony in full evening dress.

I had a vague plan to go into fashion, but I managed to keep the horror of work at arm's length by telling my parents that I wanted to become proficient in French. I spent a year in Geneva at the university there, living with a farming and wine-growing family whose land rolled all the way down to the lake. They had many refugees from Russia working in the house and on its land. The girls had ghastly stories of their treatment in Russia, terrible tales of multiple rapes, which reminded me of those cattle wagons I had seen crossing Russia at the start of the war, and all the stories of pain and terror the wagons must have contained. This caused me to reflect that, while change was all around us, and we all had to adjust, there was a vast gulf of experience between us. My war adventures were exactly that, but theirs were entirely traumatic. Nonetheless, our memories, though vastly different, would endure forever.

CHAPTER TWELVE

A DIFFERENT LIFE

Ann Mari with the dachshunds in Regents Park, 1948.

AFTER THE YEAR in Switzerland, I decided to have a brush with Bohemia and started attending art classes in Glebe Place in Chelsea. Among my fellow students was Moyra Jacobsson. We shared Sweden in common: her father was Per Jacobsson, a Swedish economist, who had worked for the League of Nations and became the director of the International Monetary Fund and naturally knew my father. He was highly regarded. When he died in 1963, John F. Kennedy wrote a letter of condolence, saying that 'the world is by far a better place to live because of Per Jacobsson's untiring efforts.'

Moyra spent a lot of time in Stockholm, and through her father, had met many Wallenbergs, whom he had known since student times. 'The Old Marcus really treated him like a son'. She had also studied in Switzerland, in Geneva, at St George's, 'a pukka English school'.

She remembers going to London after studying at the Ruskin School of Fine Art in Oxford and spending a year at the Corcoran School of Art in Washington. 'I came to London and lived in some digs in Queensgate. I am perfectly certain that my father would have checked with the Swedish ambassador or somebody similar, and asked about art schools in London. They must have said, "Oh well, the Wallenberg girl goes to Glebe Place too."'

The school was run by a painter called Bernard Adams. School is perhaps too formal a word, it was really a loose collection of classes. Like many painters who were struggling to make a living, he took in students. It was essentially a one-man show, although there were also visiting tutors. Moyra thinks there might have been a dozen or so of us studying in his studio. She remembers that, 'He knew everybody in the art world of that period. In my mind's eye I can see him sloshing down the King's Road, drunk as a coot. That didn't stop him painting pretty marvellous pictures, in my view.'

Glebe Place was a cul-de-sac, a dog leg off the King's Road, and the centre of a vibrant artistic community. Artists who were working or had worked in Glebe Place included Augustus John, Eric Gill, Winifred Nicholson, Pietro Annigoni and Francis Bacon. Walter Sickert had been at 53 Glebe Place. Charles Rennie Mackintosh designed number 49: his only London house – he had a studio at 43A.

Laurie Lee, who lived in Chelsea towards the end of the war, described the area in an essay. 'Chelsea was seedy, calm and semi-rustic at that time, with the charm of old paint and large undusted houses. Many had been deserted by their owners and were the haunt of cats and lovers, drunken soldiers on leave and sometimes all three together.'

To his eye Chelsea was still provincial, a decade and a half before the Sixties started swinging. 'The long mellow vista of terrace houses with their pavements running smooth and uncluttered, and the streets wider and clear to the eye as they were designed to be. The quiet of the country seemed to occupy the area at that time.'

Of those of us studying art at Glebe Place with Adams, only Moyra was a committed artist. 'I felt that none of the other girls – and this must have infuriated him – were there to take painting seriously. It was a holding pen for future "debs" [short for debutantes as they were called then], girls of private means, many of whom shared digs in those large Victorian flats, like a Muriel Spark novel, waiting to meet and marry Guards officers. Although I was only two or three years older, I felt not so much alienated as very different from them.

'The relief of the war being over was patent. Things were still dire in many ways, but in London, although there was the rationing, if you had enough money you could go to a restaurant. That period was still unbelievably class-ridden.' Moyra and I occasionally crossed paths at Swedish embassy parties. I also, she thinks, invited her to a party thrown by a young Swedish prince, and she was astonished that the prince helped with the washing-up. This was definitely a new post-war era.

Of all of us Moyra was the one who persevered with her art (she is still an artist, based in Oxford), and Adams put her in touch with a number of galleries: she ended up exhibiting in many of them, and at the RA. She later met and married, not a Guards officer, but Roger Bannister, the four-minute mile man.

In England, the traditional Season had started up again rather late after the war, although the strictures and grandness of the pre-War events had already been loosened. Debutantes were no longer presented in full Court Dress, but in a cocktail dress or suit – the formal Court presentations came to an end ten years later.

However there was a Season, and so I had a dance along with one of the Hambros, Theresa, the daughter of Jack Hambro, who was the head of the family. Nobody particularly liked Theresa, poor thing, including me, but I did feel a bit sorry for her. We gave a dance together.

As I was at art school I absolutely insisted on having all my art school friends along, most of whom didn't even own a dinner jacket, and some poor old dowager was also forced to have them all to dinner, to celebrate my 21st birthday. My mother had obviously completely pulled the wool over her eyes, promising her she would be hosting these fine upstanding scions of the English Establishment. Then all these Bohemians arrived, behaved frightfully badly and got tight. They were all completely drunk. Awful, really, but quite fun. My mother was furious with me for inviting them and taking advantage of this old lady.

At around this time I had my own moment of bad behaviour, when I had to go to court for attempting to smuggle a fur coat into the country. I was flying back to London from a trip to Sweden, where my father had

Ann Mari with the dachshunds again, during the art school year.

given me a fur coat. I asked if I would have to pay customs duty on it, but he dismissed that, telling me to say it was a present for my birthday, which was in fact true. When we landed I got myself into a muddle at the customs check: it was a hot day and I had the mink draped over my arm, but I messed up the story and got deeper and deeper into a tale about it being an ancient family heirloom that we had had for years. The customs men could see it was clearly brand-new. Everyone thought it was all highly amusing, and supportively told me with a good guffaw what an idiot I had been... It made the papers, which was doubly embarrassing.

The *Daily Telegraph* trumpeted, 'Banker's Daughter: She is Fined £500.' The *Evening Standard* reported that, 'Miss Ann Mari Wallenberg, 21, of Northgate, N.W. [this was our flat in St John's Wood], was fined £500 when she pleaded guilty at Uxbridge today to attempting to evade payment of Customs duty on a beaver fur coat... Mr R. Hutchings, prosecuting, said Miss Wallenberg arrived at Northolt Airport from Stockholm on

August 25 and produced a hat box and suitcase for examination. As she left the Customs shed she picked up a woollen coat and a beaver fur coat from a chair. When recalled she said the fur coat was a present given her in Sweden, and that she had brought it into the United Kingdom a year previously. She later admitted that her statement was untrue and that it had been given to her in Sweden by her father.'

My defence lawyer said on my behalf that my father had given it to me as a 21st birthday present, and that a furrier in Sweden had said he did not think I would have to pay duty on the coat. I had, said the barrister, according to the *Evening News*, 'panicked at the airport and told lies, fearing that she might lose it'.

The chairman of the magistrates, a Mr Rowland Robbins, imposing the fine said 'She has acted very stupidly.' Informed by the court that my father was a member of the Wallenberg banking family and that my stepfather a director of the Bank of England, I think their eyes lit up: the £500 fine was really quite steep, the equivalent of at least £17,000 at the time of writing...

By the time of the dance and the dinner, I was already engaged to be married, to Michael Bonsor. Michael was three years older than me. His family background reflected more than anything else the Hambro influence: Eton-educated, he was the grandson of Sir Henry Bonsor, who had been a director of the Bank of England, a Tory MP and Chairman of the brewing company Watney's and been created a Baronet in 1925. In the First World War Michael's father Robert, a Welsh Guard, was awarded a Military Cross – just like Charles Hambro. Michael himself had served in the Grenadier Guards. By coincidence Robert Bonsor was godfather to Cherry Gibbs, my friend from Queen's Gate School.

Michael and I met at an election party for the general election in February 1950. My aunt Marga had dragooned my cousin Faye and me into helping her. Marga, as political as ever, a true Mackay, was the queen bee of the Marylebone constituency. Our main job was to go to the Labour meetings and heckle: my mother turned up to one meeting dressed in a fur coat (not my notorious one) which was not a terribly good idea. I don't think she meant to: it was just cold. The left-wing were very keen on the Swedish socialist model, but she dismissed that all. 'I spent seven years in Sweden and I tell you, nobody has any imagination there. The left-wing attitude is too rigid, it kills the imagination.'

Michael had also been 'volunteered' to help. He was always interested in politics; we talked about it all the time. He was a great critic of all sides, not necessarily right-wing; in fact I think he was left-wing. There was a dinner party at some point during the campaign and we found ourselves sitting next to each other. A terribly traditional way of meeting: at least it wasn't at a pheasant shoot. Michael was a typical Etonian, which is certainly not all good, of course, but he was intelligent, that was the saving grace, and extremely musical. My mother gave us a grand piano as a wedding present and that became the centre of the houses we lived in, just as the piano had stood in the hallway at the heart of Parkudden.

Michael and I were married in July 1951. I was only just 22. We were still in the aftermath of war. My so-called trousseau was all bought with coupons, which friends and family kindly lent me. The wedding clothes were created by a Mrs Croydon of Peckham. My wedding dress was made of lace, which was not rationed, and which was all that was available unless you could get hold of some parachute silk; we tried to find some but there was none to be had.

And that was that. After my eventful childhood and teens, I became a British housewife, and mother to four children: three daughters, Celia, Charlotte and Camilla and one son, Robert. Of course we all had the usual family ups and downs – I remember Charlotte aged 16, just as we were getting on a ferry to the Isle of Wight, telling me she had been getting into some trouble at her school; I missed my footing on the gangplank, I was so shocked. It was nonetheless a settled, sedentary existence in the Home Counties of England that stood in restfully predictable, stable contrast to all the ructions and peregrinations of my first two decades.

I watched my brothers, my half-sister and step-siblings grow older, sometimes wiser, and leading their own lives. Pamela and Diana Hambro married two brothers, respectively Andrew and David Gibson-Watt,

Above: Emerging from St Peter's, Eaton Square, July 1951, married to Michael Bonsor.
Opposite top: With my father, Marcus Wallenberg, who gave me away.
Opposite below: The bridesmaids and pageboys, in traditional Swedish dress.
From left to right: Pamela Leslie-Melville, Ian Lowe, Caroline Bonsor, Richard Bonsor,
Nicola Mackay-James and Julian Gibson-Watt.

direct descendants of James Watt, who were the girls' second cousins, and who had followed the same path as so many of the Hambros and their friends: Eton, the Welsh Guards (David received a Military Cross and two bars) and Cambridge.

Andrew Gibson-Watt wrote a memoir, self-deprecatingly entitled *An Undistinguished Life*. He tells the story of how after many years he met Pammie again. She had previously married a Grenadier officer Robin Lowe (a fellow Etonian, son of the actor John Loder and stepson of Hedy Lamarr) with whom she had a son, Ian. But the marriage foundered, and she was invited to stay at Doldowlod, the Gibson-Watt house in the Wye Valley. 'It did not take very long to fall in love', he wrote.

Charles and Doie were not sure about Pammie embarking on a second marriage so soon after her first, but then the Hambros came to visit. 'It was a somewhat odd day, because I had nearly shot Sir Charles in the course of a woodcock drive. A large bald head appeared out of the wrong rhododendron bush and I don't know how I missed it.' Nonetheless Andrew and Charles become good friends, and when Pammie's divorce came through in 1951, she and Andrew were married that same June, a few days after my own wedding to Michael... 'It was a season of marriages.'

Charles Hambro died in 1963: my mother had moved out of Dixton – which my stepbrother Charlie inherited – to a flat in Cadogan Gardens, and also had a cottage called 'The Sanctuary' in Wilmington in Sussex, not far from Roedean School (she had loved being at Roedean). But if she was living a quieter life she still maintained her standards.

My niece Catharine gives this thumbnail sketch of her visits in later life: 'She was petite, immaculately dressed in a matching jacket and skirt, three strings of pearls, an emerald solitaire, a brooch and a snake bracelet (possibly a gift from Charles). She arrived in a white Triumph Stag: glamour on wheels. She had a high intellect, always very feminine, but with a seam of granite. If anyone in the house had the merest hint of a sniffle she would turn round, climb back in the Stag and head home.'

In the late 1960s Frances Partridge bumped into my mother in London and noted how much she had changed from the Doie Mackay of Newnham

A typical Wallenberg-Hambro get-together. Dinner at the Savoy in the 1950s, from left to right standing: Michael Bonsor, Charles Hambro, David Gibson-Watt, Marc Wallenberg, Michael Leslie-Melville, Charlie Hambro jr, Andrew Gibson-Watt. Seated left to right: Diana Gibson-Watt, Sally Hambro, Doie Hambro, Pammie Gibson-Watt, Ann Mari, Olga Wallenberg, Rosie Hambro and Cynthia Leslie-Melville.

days: she thought my mother was a shadow of her former self. She certainly had become more reclusive after Charles Hambro died, and she had changed. Although she remained a great reader – her homes were always awash with books – whenever I asked her if she wanted to come with me to visit Cambridge to see her old haunts she said no. What had happened to the girl who had obviously enjoyed her time there? Perhaps like most of her contemporaries at Newnham there was education but precious little opportunity for women to use their brains afterwards. The options were to pursue a Bohemian life like Frances, or marry a rich man. The latter route – and the social life that went with it – had obviously won the day for my mother.

I don't think my father ever forgave me for not marrying somebody he had chosen for me: he had always been trying to marry me off to some Swedish ballbearing magnate's son. And he certainly continued to call me and introduce me as 'Ann Mari Wallenberg', and never used my married surname Bonsor. A couple of times a year he would ring up out of the blue to ask me to come to dinner the next night, not in a London restaurant but in Stockholm. 'I'll send the tickets' was his offer. But I always told him it was the nanny's night off so I couldn't possibly get away. I think I felt I had managed to escape his often suffocating protectiveness, and was quite happy to remain outside his control. If I had stayed in Sweden I would have gone insane.

When he died in 1982, he was not buried at the Wallenberg family mausoleum near Malmvik, instead he was buried alongside his wife Marianne at his estate Vidbynäs. The funeral was immensely formal. My daughters had to wear pitch-black clothes, white collars, a diamond brooch and a veil. My own veil draped down to my waist. I was proud of not displaying grief, of remaining stoic in public. Nowadays the opposite seems to be the norm.

Although I had not seen my brothers from the moment my mother, Charles Hambro and I left Stockholm in May 1940 until after the war, whenever I did get to see them after that we always got on tremendously well. We were thrilled to see each other, because we had lost so much time. They were young men by the time they came over to England, and since they had been away at boarding school when I was in Stockholm, we barely knew each other. We talked a little about the past but only briefly; there was not much shared past to pick over.

Although my life was different, settled, and now very English, there was always a sense of continuing tradition, even if the world was radically, rapidly altering. I went up to Glencruitten every single year, staying in the Bungey. My children adored it there, running wild in the woods just as I had done. The house was exactly as it had been. Even the stairs creaked in precisely the same place. Every August the Argyllshire Gathering took place as it had each year since 1871, its highlights the Oban Games and the Ball and Dance held in the Gathering Hall on Breadalbane Street. My grandfather had been involved in building the Hall, but no one mentioned it, in that very Scottish way that it is unnecessary to draw attention to yourself and your achievements: 'No one's looking at you, dear' as the Mitfords' nanny famously remarked to Diana Mitford on her wedding day.

We would also spend the occasional Christmas at Glencruitten, and one year in the 1960s I drove up with my mother. We left at four in the morning in a huge Volvo, a good Swedish car, packed to the gunwales with provisions on the roof rack and in an enormous trailer because there was nothing to buy in Oban except Cheddar cheese, beef and potatoes. The children and the dogs were stuck in the boot. After twenty miles one of the trailer wheels fell off, and because it was Christmas nothing was open. At last we rustled someone up, got the wheel fixed, and then the clutch went wrong. Another mad journey. I took a wrong turning and couldn't back up the trailer, which meant we had to make a huge detour. All the while Mama was telling me what a terrible idea it all was. We arrived at Glencruitten, to be met at the door by the butler, Johnnie, the fires all lit, a warm welcome; what a relief. Johnnie was Glencruitten at its best.

My Scottish relations seemed to cruise on regardless, and kept to their unyielding schedule of spending April to October in Scotland, and the dark winter months in Florida. They went on ignoring the shifting times and, in Scotland, the pouring rain: hunting, shooting and changing for dinner until the day they died, or playing tennis and diving off the boathouse roof into the waters of Lake Rochelle when in Florida. My first cousin Tad (or Weenie), the daughter of Ferrier and Grace, dressed for dinner every night, no matter what climate she was in. Her Martini came in on a tray at six o'clock sharp. I can see her floating down the stairs to collect it. She was a great, tragic beauty, like a character from a Tennessee Williams play.

However, even unchanging times had to change. Tad's sister, one of my other first cousins, Ba (Elizabeth), had inherited both the Scottish and Florida estates and after she died, Glencruitten was left to her son Max

Mackay-James. The Florida estate was sold and so Tad, who by this time largely lived in a world of her own, began spending the whole year in Scotland. Even into her seventies, the ice and snow thrilled her – she, who had never probably witnessed the frozen cold. Many was the time when I and my children delighted to see her, well into her seventies, toboggan down the snow-covered slopes of the Glencruitten gardens on a tea-tray.

Eventually, even Glencruitten had to be sold – in the early 2000s – and its contents auctioned. I had wanted to buy either some lovely turquoise pots from the library, or the octagonal table from the library anteroom, the one which had the bronze statue of Isadora Duncan on top, because they held such strong childhood memories, but they all went for too much. Instead, I bought one of the Lorimer light fittings, which is still in my house near Newbury, half buried in one of the ceilings – it is so huge that only a few bulbous bits stick out at the bottom – but at least there is a piece of Glencruitten for me to see every day.

Although that magical house is no longer in the family, the lands around it are, and one element of Glencruitten continues to flourish. The Cathedral of Trees remains as a monument to Alexander Mackay's vision.

In 1921 he imagined, and planted out, a living Cathedral of Trees, both as a memorial to the First World War, and a way of providing employment for returning veterans. My aunt Marga, with her forestry studies and agricultural training, helped him. Its plan was laid out in the form, and to the same scale, of St Andrew's Cathedral in Glasgow, complete with a cloister, 'choir stalls' of golden yew, a 'High Altar' of cotoneaster, windows of purple beech and prunus, and thick walls of beech, spruce, chestnuts and limes. From Arizona, fossilised tree stumps were shipped in. He simultaneously created a similar cathedral of eucalyptus trees at his Florida estate at Lake Alfred. When Alexander died in 1936 he was buried in the Cathedral of Trees at Glencruitten: his headstone carried a verse from Isaiah 32: 'And a man shall be a hiding place from the wind and a covert from the temple, as rivers of water in a dry place, as the shadow of a great rock in a weary land.' His wife Edith, and daughter Elizabeth (Aunty Pooh) are buried with him at the high altar. In the 'side chapels' are many tablets commemorating other members of the family.

The location Alexander selected was in a valley looking towards Ben Cruachan, in low, boggy ground next to a small loch, which in the long term made it increasingly difficult to maintain the Cathedral. It became overgrown and many of the hedges were withering, until two of his other great-grandchildren, my cousins Susanah and Nicola, set up a charity to restore it to his original splendour.

The Glencruitten Cathedral of Trees is a place designed for quiet reflection. As I now reflect on those strands running through my life, the Scottish, the Swedish, the English, the 'bloody neutral', perhaps a fitting end is a phrase my cousin Nicola once said about Alexander, that 'a man who plants trees has an eye on eternity'. That, I think, is an excellent sentiment.

The Cathedral of Trees in its early incarnation in the grounds of the Glencruitten Estate.

INDEX

ACKNOWLEDGEMENTS

Ann Mari died on 29th April 2019, shortly after completing this book, and while this is a cause of great sadness to all who knew and loved her, her story survives, for posterity.

Many parents refused to send their children abroad during the War, and the majority who did were not from such comfortable backgrounds. There may, understandably, be less sympathy for Ann Mari's narrative, yet it offers an insight to a pre-War economic and banking network where close relationships were forged across continents. These families were engaged in top secret, high-level negotiations for their respective governments, which meant that their children were at risk as soon as hostilities broke out.

This, one of the last, verbatim accounts of a life lived during the upheavals of war would not have been possible without the help and support of the following: Ann Mari's daughters Celia Pilkington, Charlotte Milln and Camilla Bonsor; the book's author, Philip Dodd, who spent many – as he says – enjoyable hours with her, transcribing her words, fact-checking and researching the archives; The Wallenberg Foundation, whose generous support and picture library has been invaluable; Susanah Mackay-James and Sally, Viscountess Hampden for various family images; Bernard Higton who has patiently designed the book pages, creating the elegant layouts you see here.

For their kindness in sharing their memories and making available important research materials, many thanks to: Moyra Bannister & Charlotte Bannister-Parker; Pamela Gibson-Watt; Jane Hoare; Pamela Hunter, Archivist at C. Hoare & Co.; Dr Patricia McGuire, Archivist at King's College, Cambridge; John Adams Morgan & Chauncey Morgan; Cherry Palmer (née Gibbs), Robert M. Pennoyer; Caroline Särnqvist at Sveriges Kungahus; Julia Schmidt at the Churchill Archives Centre; Anne Thomson, Archivist at Newnham College, Cambridge; Connie White; the AELTC archives, Wimbledon.